Love, Sex and Long-Term Relationships

by the same author

Asperger Syndrome – A Love Story
Sarah Hendrickx and Keith Newton
Foreword by Tony Attwood
ISBN 978 1 84310 540 4

Asperger Syndrome and Employment
What People with Asperger Syndrome Really Really Want
Sarah Hendrickx
ISBN 978 1 84310 677 7

of related interest

The Complete Guide to Asperger's Syndrome
Tony Attwood
ISBN 978 1 84310 495 7

Asperger's Syndrome and Sexuality
From Adolescence through Adulthood
Isabelle Hénault
Foreword by Tony Attwood
ISBN 978 1 84310 189 5

Sex, Sexuality and the Autism Spectrum
Wendy Lawson
Foreword by Glenys Jones
ISBN 978 1 84310 284 7

Aspergers in Love
Maxine Aston
Foreword by Gisela Slater-Walker
ISBN 978 1 84310 115 4

An Asperger Marriage
Gisela and Christopher Slater-Walker
Foreword by Tony Attword
ISBN 978 1 84310 017 1

Asperger Syndrome and Long-Term Relationships
Ashley Stanford
Foreword by Liane Holliday Willey
ISBN 978 1 84310 734 7

Asperger Syndrome and Employment
Adults Speak Out about Asperger Syndrome
Edited by Genevieve Edmonds and Luke Beardon
ISBN 978 1 84310 648 7
Adults Speak Out about Asperger Syndrome series

Love, Sex and Long-Term Relationships

What People with Asperger Syndrome Really Really Want

Sarah Hendrickx

Foreword by Stephen Shore

Jessica Kingsley Publishers
London and Philadelphia

First published in 2008
by Jessica Kingsley Publishers
116 Pentonville Road
London N1 9JB, UK
and
400 Market Street, Suite 400
Philadelphia, PA 19106, USA

www.jkp.com

Library of Congress Cataloging in Publication Data
Hendrickx, Sarah.
   Love, sex and long-term relationships : what people with asperger syndrome really really want /
Sarah Hendrickx ; foreword by Stephen Shore.
      p. cm.
   ISBN 978-1-84310-605-0 (pb : alk. paper) 1.   Asperger's syndrome—Patients—Sexual
behavior. 2. Asperger's syndrome—Social aspects. I. Title.
   RC553.A88H463 2008
   616.85'8832—dc22

                                        2007033013

British Library Cataloguing in Publication Data
A CIP catalogue record for this book is available from the British Library

ISBN 978 1 84310 605 0

Printed and bound in Great Britain by
MGP Books Group, Cornwall

Contents

Foreword

Often shrouded in secrecy and shame, sexuality and intimate relationships can be a difficult topic to just talk about, never mind to research. For people with Asperger Syndrome these challenges are magnified still further due to myths and misconceptions of how we relate to others. However, Sarah Hendrickx has masterfully taken the vastly under-researched area of Asperger Syndrome and sexuality. By directly interviewing people on the autistic spectrum and non-spectrum partners, Sarah has smashed the old theories of sexuality in areas such as desire, masturbation, quantity, emotions (or lack of same), and brought understanding of intimate relations of people with Asperger Syndrome to new heights.

Sarah's research indicates that although there are differences between those with Asperger Syndrome and the rest of the population, many things remain the same. For example, for those able to do so, the standard advice of circulating in the community bodes well for everyone seeking to expand their social network with the possibility of developing intimate relations with others.

Liking to be asked questions about themselves turned out to be universally favoured by people both on and off the autistic spectrum. We find another commonality between people on both sides of the spectrum in that guidance from the partner on how to help and support is almost always good for a relationship. Making adjustments based on understanding is good too. Additionally, being free to make requests is important. The 'universals' are often just amplified for people on the autistic spectrum.

I believe that for me, being on the autistic spectrum may actually help my marriage, as it is automatically assumed by both my wife and I that the stereotypical 'mind reading' type of communication that allegedly goes on between couples must be replaced by discussion and checking in with each other's needs and preferences. Just like any other couple, we have fallen into our roles of speciality. For example, my systematising skills help with areas such as finances and planning for trips. My wife's finely tuned abilities to read social situations allow her to act as an ambassador to the non-spectrum world for me, thus empowering me to achieve greater social inclusion.

For me, and many others on the autistic spectrum, particular attention needs to be paid to the environment. For example, whereas a bar may be a place for many to meet others, for me, those venues often are a basketful of sensory violations and can be overwhelming even without taking into account having to read numerous non-verbal cues. Speaking of sensory issues, they turned out to be a concern for over 80 per cent of people on the autistic spectrum in terms of relationships and intimate reactions. As Sarah indicated in her book, one female with AS reports "lik[ing] rougher stimulation…my neck sucked…[being] bit, [and] slapped." Knowledge of sensory differences can help the partner possibly reframe these preferences to hypo-sensitivities rather than the more commonly assumed sadomasochism.

For example, while smells are important to me and my relationship with my non-spectrum wife, her aversion to perfumes works very well for us. Even the smell of sweat is preferable to me than perfume. Deep, strong pressure is welcomed whereas light touch is an aversive for me. Communication is vital for my wife to understand these things.

This book is chock full of helpful explanations as to the dynamics of intimate relationships combined with what can often be relationship-saving tips helping to promote greater understanding. Whether it is seeking out others, socialising or maintaining harmony in a relationship we find that people with Asperger Syndrome run the gauntlet of emotions, desires and preferences just like everyone else – perhaps just more so. Thank you Sarah for opening a doorway into a greater understanding of intimate relations for everyone, and for a fuller experience on what it is like to be human.

Stephen M. Shore, EdD
Board of Directors for the Asperger's Association of New England
author of Beyond the Wall: Personal Experiences with Autism and Asperger Syndrome *co-author of* Understanding Autism for Dummies

1

Introduction

This book seeks to explore the experiences of adults with Asperger Syndrome (AS) within the realms of sex, gender and relationships. Primarily, this work is for those with AS. Sex is sometimes a personal subject, which can be hard to discuss and difficult to share – for anyone. If, added to this, you have a small or non-existent peer group, it can be impossible to establish if your desires, feelings and practices are 'normal' or even acceptable, because there is no one to share with or ask. Given that some people with AS are intensely private and do not share information willingly, this can exacerbate the difficulty. Someone with AS may wonder: How do I know if others with AS experience the same discomforts or pleasures? If I cannot compare myself to the neuro-typical (NT) population, which I do not feel an affinity to, how do I know if I am the only one who feels this way? How do I find a partner if I have no one to ask how to do it? Do others feel the same anxiety, fear and loneliness? Do others feel joy and contentment in their own company?

What are the motivations behind relationship choices and sexual behaviour? Are they very different for those with AS than for anyone else? Does having extreme sensitivity to physical touch or low self-esteem change one's perception of one's sexual experience? Knowing why someone does what they do is the key to acceptance and understanding – both of the self and of others.

Although more is now known and reported about relationships involving one or both partners with AS, little has been written about the thoughts and experiences of those with the condition. Fortunately, the old adage that people with autism don't have relationships or get married has been well and truly jettisoned, because this is far from the truth. From my work and that of others, it is apparent that those with autism, and particularly AS, have as wide a range of desires and needs as anyone, but may have more difficulty in realising them due to limited social contact and less developed interaction skills. It is not surprising, then, that some people decide not to bother with relationships at all. For some the idea of having to comprehend another's needs as being different from one's own, and having to share space, bodily contact and emotional intimacy, is just too much to manage. For others, the decision to remain single is a positive choice, which enables them to focus their energies on other areas of their lives. For yet another sector of the AS community, a relationship is desirable and tolerable, but may still come with considerable difficulties and misunderstandings. For the partners of those with AS, there may be a confusion about the specific routines and behaviours (or the lack of) that affect the relationship. As with anyone, the range of lifestyles is broad and reflects society as a whole, but are there aspects of AS which make certain relationship experiences and decisions more commonplace?

I hope to take a step onwards from previous writing in this area (Aston 2003; Hénault 2006) and enlarge the picture of this group of people. My purpose is to share information in order to enable adults with AS to identify with others and therefore feel less alone in their thoughts. This is a particular issue for people who have few opportunities to discuss anything, let alone an intimate subject like sexuality. It is also intended that general learning for partners, professionals and families will be increased and that greater understanding and acceptance of the motivations for certain sexual choices will be gained. No judgement is made.

It is hoped, too, that, as well as benefiting those with AS in learning about their peers, this book will add to the body of knowledge of this group in order to stimulate further research, awareness and acceptance. It will also go to show that those with AS are often no different from the rest of the population in many ways.

The contents of the book examine typical issues that one may expect to encounter with a person with AS (e.g. communication, understanding the needs of another person and sensory sensitivity) and are backed up with comments from individuals to give them real-life context.

The views expressed here are mostly gleaned from requests via forums and message boards on the internet, together with some people known to me personally. Those who responded to my request completed a questionnaire and were asked if they would be willing to correspond further. Respondents were provided with information regarding the rationale for the book, and a guarantee of confidentiality and anonymity. Surprisingly, given the sensitive nature of the questions, most people were happy to answer the original questions and often more. The general tone of communication was that this area was under-researched and that people were willing to contribute in any way they could in order to increase awareness. I was encouraged by the enormous enthusiasm with which my request was received. I was available for further questions and information on this topic as a token 'payment' for the time given to the questions. All respondents were sent a summary of findings from the analysis of the questionnaires.

Responses came from single people with AS, those in relationships and also their partners – some with AS, some without. Some participants were self-diagnosed, others had an 'official' diagnosis. Of all the respondents, only one had been aware of their condition prior to adulthood, so most had not had the benefit of AS-specific support during childhood. Over 50 per cent were over 30 years of age when AS entered their lives, and so had endured many years of adulthood without knowing their true identity. It will be interesting, in the future, to see if relationship profiles change as we see an increasing adult population who have had early diagnoses of AS and early support and understanding. Given the issues regarding diagnosis in adults and the difficulty in obtaining one (on the NHS, in the UK), it was decided that, if someone declared themselves to have AS, then their judgement would be respected, assuming that no one would bother to state such a thing without fair reason. Respondents' comments have been identified with their standpoint in brackets (AS/NT), where appropriate.

The research sample is somewhat small: made up of 36 men with AS, four women with AS and 27 NT women, who are or have been partners of people with AS. All the heterosexual women with AS were in relationships with men with AS. One lesbian couple were an NT/AS partnership. No NT men or gay men, either NT or AS, responded. Not all the respondents answered all the questions – this is reflected in the percentages or data given – and some information was provided by partners on behalf of each other. Other quotes have been used from other writers with AS, and these have been used with permission and referenced where appropriate.

As some of these quotes are taken out of their original context, they have been presented anonymously; similarly, all other respondents remain unidentified. Permission has been obtained from the authors to use their contributions, for which I am grateful. No claims or generalisations of behaviour are made. These are some experiences and thoughts of a small section of the AS population, and/or their partners.

There is a wide age range of participants, from early 20s to 70s, and notice is drawn to different expectations and general societal differences for individuals growing up and engaging partners in different decades. There may have been fewer social expectations in the past and finding willing partners may have been easier, or perhaps gender roles were more defined with males expected to be making the first move and females having to wait to be asked. The answers to these questions depend on culture, environment and personality as much as they do on AS, but it is as well to be aware that this group, like any other, is not a homogeneous one.

It is acknowledged that those who have responded may be a certain type of person – that is, those who visit support websites of are already in relationships; therefore, this is not a representative population sample. I felt that due to the nature of the topic and my inability to provide adequate support for more vulnerable people with AS, I should not contact organisations which provide residential or more intensive support, although such a group may have provided a different outlook on the subject.

I also acknowledge that I was frustratingly unable to gain motivations for some behaviour either because this was contributed as an experience of a partner or because I was unable to have enough contact with the respondent to discuss the particular thread. I have erred on the side of caution so as not to 'push my luck' or offend.

The book assumes a basic knowledge of AS and does not go into the diagnostic criteria in detail. There are many websites and resources which do this. *The Complete Guide to Asperger Syndrome* by Tony Attwood (2006) is the most comprehensive of these to date.

I write as a freelance trainer and worker with adults with AS and also as a partner of a man with AS. My partner and I have discussed our own relationship in our previous book, *Asperger Syndrome – A Love Story* (Hendrickx and Newton 2007). I do not presume to know how those with AS feel and experience the world because I do not have AS myself, but have spent a large amount of time with many individuals who do have AS and I hope to share some non-AS insights along with the comments of those questioned.

For further information on training, support and consultancy services for individuals and couples affected by Asperger Syndrome and autism, please visit www.asperger-training.com.

I am very grateful to all those who willingly agreed to answer personal questions and took the time to respond to my requests for more of the same, particularly to Ron, Matthew and Keith who gave more than most. I was encouraged by the responses of some couples who had found the process of asking and answering intimate questions as a couple a beneficial experience to their own relationships, and I am pleased that this work has been useful already. The main purpose of writing this book is to provide greater understanding and knowledge for individuals with AS and also for those who support them either personally or professionally. Thank you to all who contributed. I hope I have done your experiences justice.

2

Finding a Partner

As might be expected of individuals who by definition have issues with social interaction, communication, adapting to change and comprehending the needs of others, all aspects of finding, establishing and maintaining a relationship are potentially problematic for individuals with Asperger Syndrome (AS). When we also consider other possible differences in motor skills and sensory experiences, the likelihood of confusion and difficulty increases. Despite all these obstacles, many people with AS express a strong desire to investigate relationships and sexual experiences, and some are very successful at it. Others find the whole thing much harder and may feel despondent when things don't go according to plan. These feelings of not being able to find a compatible partner are not limited to the AS population: they are a feature of adult life generally. The magnitude of the perceived failure may be harder for someone with AS to manage because they may have fewer social contacts with whom to talk about what went wrong. There may also be a greater tendency to ruminate or see things in a black and white way, and they may find it hard to keep things in perspective. It is useful to remember that having a partner is only a part of a full and interesting life, and is sometimes more difficult than being alone.

There appears to be no significant difference in the onset of puberty or in the age at which young people with AS become interested in sexual relations in comparison to the general population (Hénault 2006). It is other factors that determine the success of their endeavours. The whole business of sexuality and interpersonal relations is confusing and fraught with complex and subtle intentions that require decoding (Hénault 2006).

This chapter will focus on how people are finding and choosing potential partners, and it will include comments about how their experiences have affected them.

Where to look

An initial difficulty may be that someone with AS has a more limited social network than a neuro-typical (NT) person. Some people with AS have no one whom they could describe as a 'friend' and, given that any social opportunity is a possible chance of meeting someone, the fewer the social contacts, the fewer the invitations and the fewer the possibilities of finding a partner. We live in a social world full of signs and signals, and assumptions that everyone understands all these. The majority of NT people do understand most of them, but they still get confused and often make mistakes when reading other people. NT individuals have fairly efficient non-verbal skills in infancy and then hone these with constant practice throughout their lifetime. The less developed early social skills of an AS person results in a lifelong lack of practice and hence a continued disadvantage when compared to NT peers – if you can't gain entry into the social arena, you can't remain in there to improve your skills. Not knowing how to approach someone, what to say and how to respond to approaches made to you are common occurrences for those with AS, and this makes the whole relationship game a nerve-wracking experience. In fact, it is fairly scary for anyone, but some NT people have a head start in social skills and making small talk.

Typical places for people to meet new people are either in social settings such as bars, at parties or at work. Many adults with AS are unemployed or under-employed in positions that do not reflect their academic capabilities, and so are not in an appropriate workplace for a 'meeting of minds'. Those who are employed at the level of their abilities tend to work in AS-friendly environments such as science, engineering and the IT industries – environments which may attract other people with limited social skills and hence be less likely to be a highly social environment! As it has been suggested that the best partner for someone with AS is someone else with AS (Grandin 1996), this could be perfect. It just takes someone to make the first move:

I asked (friend's name) to advise me in methods of ultimately getting a girlfriend. Essentially she said, 'You need to get out of the lab'. I never gave any thought to the time I spend in my laboratory – my own little world, perfect for an Aspie. I am starting small – eating lunch in the food court rather than at my desk. Even though I still sit alone in the food court, there is the opportunity for someone to sit with me. (AS male, engineer)

The internet has been great for many people who don't want to, or are unable to, go and meet people in face-to-face group social settings. The autistic community has embraced the written medium of the web, which doesn't require body language and confusing social rules and instead focuses on what is actually being said or written. There are huge numbers of web forums, message boards and sites specifically for those with an autistic spectrum condition and those who spend their lives with them – parents, partners, etc. An internet search for 'asperger' plus other appropriate words uncovers a wealth of online activity. This has enabled people to redefine the terms of friendship and relationships. People may be close friends and confidants, without even having seen or met each other, and spend hours chatting and communicating in great personal depth. Other people have 'virtual' sexual relationships with people via the internet, which removes the need for social conversation and provides sexual relief in an easy, emotion-free, physical contact-free environment, which is perfect for some. Times they are a-changing.

There are also many online dating sites for the general world at large and this is perhaps the ideal medium for helping the person with AS to find a partner. Care should be taken to select an appropriate site for the requirements of the individual. Some dating sites are for those who are searching for long-term partners and others are more for casual sexual encounters. It is useful to ensure that there are enough members in your locality if the intention is to meet other people. Most sites offer a trial search before joining up, although they rarely allow any contact with members until after joining and there is usually a fee. There are also AS/autism dating and friendship sites (e.g. Aspie Affection and Aspie Friends) to ensure that a disclosure of your AS will not be met with rejection or a lack of understanding, and that any prospective partner will be happy to meet someone with those specific autistic qualities.

When initiating or responding to any contact, whether online or in person, it is important that all parties concerned understand what the nature of the relationship is to be – whether friendship, casual sex or potentially a future serious relationship. It is not necessary to do this at the first contact – and not a good idea as you may be accused of rushing things or being too intense – but after a few meetings it may be a good idea to find out what the other person's intentions and feelings are, because they may be different from your own. Failure to do this could result in misunderstanding and serious consequences – if one person believes the relationship to be potentially sexual and the other doesn't, any physical or sexual approaches may be unwelcome and received with anger and rejection. This is the case for all relationships, no matter how they begin. It is generally accepted in the NT population that one should just 'know' what the intention of the other party is by reading the signals. Obviously, this is not always possible for those with AS, and it is also difficult for most people without AS who often get it wrong all the time. Asking questions as to the nature of the relationship may be seen as inherently unromantic and embarrassing. Explaining the features of AS may help to get the understanding of a partner, because most NT people will not ask those questions – they will just try and guess what the feelings of the other person are for fear of looking foolish by having to ask.

The advantages of internet dating are that one is not judged on first impressions as one would be in a bar or club. This is helpful to the person with AS who typically is not at their most comfortable in social or group situations. People can build up relationships with others through emails, phone calls and messaging, so that when the first meeting occurs there may be enough shared history and attraction to overcome any initial awkwardness:

> Internet dating is the ideal medium: it allows pre-selection filtering, and because in the early stages it mostly involves relatively anonymous forms of communication (email), the gaucheness (physical, spoken, appearance) isn't so pervasive in the eye (mind) of the recipient. This reduces the chances of being dismissed immediately. (AS male)

It is advisable to look through other profiles of members on the site to get an idea of what to write when compiling your own profile. One man with AS, when being supported to write an online profile, was asked what type of person he was looking for and said: 'I don't mind; anyone really'. While this may be honest, it is not what a person reading an online profile wants to hear – they will want to feel that they have been specially chosen and are individually attractive. Research, trial and error can be a good means of building an attractive and interesting profile on a dating site. Getting help from someone else is often useful because it can be difficult to judge your own strengths and attractive qualities. Many dating sites have tips pages which are a useful reference. This idea of presenting selected information can be particularly problematic for someone with AS, who may have a need for privacy or want to be entirely honest. It is important to present a realistic profile of yourself, while choosing what to reveal.

One man with AS wrote on his internet dating profile that he was a recovering alcoholic. While this is courageous and honest, it may also deter some people from making contact because they may perceive him to be a person with problems. If he had given them this information after they had got to know him, it may not have had such a strong effect. For this person, this was an active decision: he felt that he had been through so much and that anyone who was put off by his disclosure would not be someone that he would want a relationship with anyway. The decision on how much to disclose and at what stage is an individual one:

> I was looking on the internet. I wanted to be wanted. It is interesting, fun and exciting to be around someone. I also wanted sex. (AS male)

One woman explained how her AS partner had gone to detailed efforts in order to find a suitable partner before meeting her. His first sexual partner in his late 30s is now his wife. She says:

> He tried everything! Dating friends, blind dates, using classifieds, phone dating services…singles chat rooms. Buying tons of how to date books and going to the places those books recommended. He was methodical about dating. He kept a chart for his college years. In this chart he

had information like who initiated the contact, how many times they had gone out, what was the put-off... He also kept the voice messages of people he met over dating services that had any comments about him. The message which hooked me was a perfect message which took more than six years of charts and analysis to produce. So he took many pains to study his negative experiences; he did not want to be alone. (NT female)

For the NT partner, the internet can be a safe means of vetting potential partners and they may find the person with AS unusually articulate and less overtly sexual, which can be a refreshing change from some non-AS people (Aston 2003). Those with AS can be especially adept and charming via the written word. Several non-AS partners commented about the demeanour of their partner online and their voice over the phone, prior to meeting:

His (AS) voice! He has the most wonderful voice. (NT female)

For those who have an active social life, church groups, college and work were noted as being places where people had met their partners. Clubs and bars were rarely cited as the places respondents met potential partners – AS or not.

As one of the factors identified in attraction in a partner was shared interests, it may be useful to identify places and pursuits that are of interest to others. Groups, classes and clubs that involve your specific interest may be good places to meet others who enjoy the same activities. While turning up for the first time can be nerve-wracking, it may be the start of a new social life. It is important not to see these occasions as primarily a place to meet partners, but as opportunities to expand life experience, practise socialising and learn new things. There may be no one at the group who is attractive or available but each one of the other members will have friends, families and other contacts among whom there may be a perfect partner! Every new person in one's existing social network is a link to a whole new social network.

Selection

Those with AS may have specific preferences as to their choice of partner and the internet provides background information in the form of dating profiles that allow pre-selection. This may suit the logical mindset of some people with AS who may be more motivated by shared interests or lifestyle choices than by notions of 'chemistry'. Be aware that dating can become a fascination and an all-encompassing interest. While you may feel that you have a special relationship with someone online, they may be corresponding with a number of other people and see things as being more casual. It is wise to take things slowly and not become too intense too quickly. It should be remembered that a profile is only the beginning of a person's personality and that asking questions and getting to know them takes some time. It is also worth considering communicating with people who have different interests from your own. This may be an opportunity to learn something new and broaden your own sphere of knowledge and understanding. It also provides new topics that you can both discuss and ask each other questions about. People like to be asked about themselves. It makes them feel that they are interesting and special. The internet was cited by many respondents as their main means of meeting partners.

Some people with AS may have physical preferences for a potential partner, such as hair or eye colour, and these can be selected online. It can be useful to be able to look at someone in a photograph and not have the pressure of immediately having to engage with them socially in person. However, photographs are not always a clear representation of how a person will be – they may have cut their hair, be wearing different clothes or it may not be a very recent photograph.

Several people with AS, when asked, said that the main attracting feature of a potential partner was whether that person liked them. Maxine Aston notes in *Asperger's in Love* (2003, p.16) that: 'being liked, approved of and needed appeared very important'. The person with AS may have low self-esteem and feel that they have no right to show their attraction to someone they like. This may be the result of a lifetime of negative feedback from social situations and a lack of successful interactions with people. Over 90 per cent of those with AS will have been bullied at some point (Attwood 2006, p.98) and this can result in a lack of self-worth and an inability to believe that anyone would have an interest in them:

> By early teens I was aware that others had an interest in each other. There was interest in me – I was asked to school discos. By that point I didn't trust anyone as general behaviour from others had always been negative. Almost all interaction between me and others was to make a mockery of me. Why would this new interest be any different? (AS male)

It may also be a logical decision – why bother to be interested in someone if they have no interest in me and nothing will come of it? This may be seen as a waste of energy and irrational. Further into the relationship, the person with AS may still evaluate their sense of worth from what their partner tells them (Aston 2003). For many NT people, there is often a more active choosing of a partner and the decision as to whether they are attractive is made very quickly after meeting and is not dependent on whether the attraction is reciprocated. Some NT people will pursue a person whom they like despite being told that the feelings are not mutual. 'Connection' and 'chemistry' are words that describe the feelings some people feel immediately upon meeting someone they like:

> I knew that they found me attractive, so that I wouldn't have to try and be someone that I'm not. (AS male)

> Initially anyone who likes me is enough, as time goes by selection occurs and if it doesn't feel right, I leave. I don't feel worthy to make my intentions known without the other person expressing an interest first. (AS male)

> I understand he (AS) never approaches anyone that isn't interested in him. (NT female)

> What is the point in liking someone who is not interested? (AS male)

> She seemed interested in me. I got married because I thought that's what people are supposed to do. (AS male)

A variety of other important aspects have been reported by those with AS in terms of what is attractive in a partner, including physical appearance and personality. Sex is not often mentioned as a primary reason for selecting a partner (Aston 2003). Hair was a common preference:

> Extrovert, long hair, linked into the world socially in a way that I wasn't. (AS male)

> I find intelligence highly attractive and also short hair, for some reason! Most of my partners have ended up with short hair after going out with me for any length of time. (AS male)

> Physical looks just long enough to get the conversation going. (AS female)

> Physical attractiveness is definitely what piques my interest. I cannot be partnered with someone I do not find attractive. (AS male)

> Any woman with too much make-up and/or extravagant hair and/or long fingernails seems very shallow to me. I want a woman who, similar to me, highlights the details of her world, not the details of her body. (AS male)

Lianne Holliday Willey, a female writer who has AS, talks about the aesthetics of her husband's face (2005, p.90):

> In the structure of his face, I see so many of the visual elements that appeal to me – linear lines, symmetry, straightness, perfect alignments… It is a visual respite for me.

Finding a partner who does not cause too much stress and extra effort seems to be important to those with AS and someone who can aid social inclusion with their better developed social skills. A partner who can easily slot into the AS person's existing lifestyle can increase their relationship potential. The person may already be at full capacity with managing their own daily life, and simply would rather remain alone than take on the seemingly complex and overwhelming requirements of shared life with another person. This is not necessarily the case for some

NT people who have the capacity to manage a lot of social contact with others and may not need to maintain sameness and routines in their lives. It is likely that there will be an expectation that life will change when you are in a relationship, and that the new partner will take priority over previously preferred activities and time. Failing to allow this will cause your partner to feel that they are unimportant because they may show a preference for people (you) over their activities or interests:

> He had an interest in virtually all of my favourite activities, even my favourite pastime that no one else had ever expressed an interest in. (AS female)

> Beauty, attitude, being the exact opposite of me. Need someone who will refine me, make me less Aspie. (AS male)

> Long-term important traits – understanding, appreciation, enough overlap, enough difference. (AS male)

> Personality would probably be the most important of all factors in the long term. (AS male)

> Easy to talk to. I do not form relationships easily. (AS male)

> She (AS) is not as needy as other women, not as high maintenance. (AS male)

One woman was very clear as to her reasons for selecting her (now former) husband:

> As a teen I chose partners randomly. I chose my husband because he had some amazing gym equipment I wanted to use. (AS female)

As for partners of AS people, gentleness was the most quoted attracting aspect of their AS partner. Tony Attwood (2006, p.304) describes men with AS as having an 'effeminate' rather than 'macho' quality, which he describes as the ideal partner for the modern woman. Isabelle Hénault (2006) also describes camp mannerisms in heterosexual AS men. Quite why this seems to be the case is unclear, although women with AS have a tendency to be more masculine and 'tomboyish' than other women (Ingudomnukul *et al.* 2007).

Many women also reported how good-looking their AS partners were. Tony Attwood (2006, p.304) reports that children with AS often have angelic faces and may grow up with symmetrical facial features which, when combined with a child-like vulnerability and outlook, are appealing to certain types of women who are said to be good nurturers and empathisers. Women with AS can also have very child-like faces, although some can appear quite intense and serious because they often smile less and do not engage socially in the same way as other women, particularly in social smiling and eye contact. This can be more unexpected in a woman than in a man and provoke a stronger response in others. Generally, women with AS are seen either as vulnerable and naïve or as strong and capable by partners. Barbara Jacobs, in *Loving Mr Spock* (2006, p.17) says: 'He (AS) had the face of a cherub, the focused intelligence of a professor and the...emotional immaturity of a three-year-old'.

Some of the respondents in our study commented:

> I thought he (AS) was some kind of Buddhist; he was so self-sufficient and didn't seem to need the social approval that most people do. He was happy walking and cycling alone and living a self-contained life. I was in awe of this and thought he was amazing. (NT female)

> All round he (AS) is very good-looking. (NT female)

> Gentle, articulate, different, intellectual. (NT female)

> My husband (AS) is funny, intelligent, honest and values monogamy. After dating some less than honest or sincere men, I really valued these qualities in my husband. (NT female)

> The relationship was initiated by me. I had heard about this interesting and intelligent fellow (AS) that spent a lot of time alone up in his room playing guitar and painting. (NT female)

> Funny, gentle, not overly 'macho'. He (AS) was very fashion-challenged among other things and I saw him as a 'project'! (NT female)

Both men and women with AS can have an innocence and naïvety about them socially, which seems to contradict the often wide knowledge and expertise that the person has in intellectual areas. This can create an intriguing character, which can be unusual and interesting. Most of the AS males who responded to the questionnaire were in relationships with non-AS females, while all the heterosexual AS females were in relationships with AS males. This replicates the findings from previous research on this topic (Aston 2003). It is suggested that, while men with AS seek someone who can compensate for their areas of social and organisational weakness and select a partner at the opposite end of the empathy scale (Baron-Cohen 2003), women with AS are more likely to select a partner who is similar in terms of expectations and lifestyle choices (Attwood 2006).

Making an approach

Despite the obvious difficulties that many people with AS experience, some express a determination to find a partner. It is apparent that this is often mentally stressful, but the drive to do so seems to overcome these anxieties:

> I approached every new relationship with the same naïve and vague optimism. (AS male)

> Not knowing I was Aspie, and not really understanding behaviour or friendship very well made it easy to repeat past mistakes. I had to learn by making mistakes. (AS male)

> I used to take Valium (tranquillisers) before having sex with a partner for the first time. I had a fear of being unable to excite my partner and this enabled me to relax and enjoy myself. I only needed it the first time, after that I was OK. (AS male)

> It is definitely easier to stay alone, but I have finally mustered the courage to at least attempt a relationship. I am tired of being lonely. (AS male)

Respondents were asked whether self-esteem had played any part in their ability to begin or maintain relationships, and whether fear of failure inhibited new attempts to find someone. Someone's capacity to recover from past failures and move forward varies enormously from person to person. Self-esteem, for most people, is developed through interaction and feedback from others (Hénault 2006) and this is often lacking in those with AS because they have few opportunities to experience positive relationships. The result of this is a continuing downward spiral of negativity:

> I fear rejection, real or imaginary. (AS male)

> I come across as weird and I have a lot of chaos and responsibility in my life. I can't see anyone wanting to deal with that. (AS female)

> I could not get myself up to even asking for the better part of five years. I felt inadequate. (AS male)

> I became phobic of any women I was seriously attracted to. This condition prevented me from basically ever being in a romantic relationship. (AS male)

> I generally feel inferior to other people and therefore do not feel worthy of associating with them. (AS male)

> He (AS) did have problems with trying again after his first marriage. He was alone for ten years. (NT female)

> Compliments do not increase my self-confidence. I don't believe them to be true so they have no meaning to me. (AS male)

> Yes (fear of failure affects ability to attempt a relationship) I would still be alone if I was not set up on a blind date. (AS male)

During different periods of my life I felt so trapped by fear of sexual failure and inadequacy. The advent of Viagra® made a huge difference, as did some therapy. (AS male)

The role of alcohol and/or drugs

For a small proportion of the men with AS (14%), alcohol or drugs played a large part in their ability to manage the anxiety that is often inherent in the condition. This was not mentioned by any women with AS. Those who said they regularly drank alcohol or took drugs had the highest number of sexual partners within AS men – at least eight partners, with most commenting on having 'numerous' partners. This was far higher than the average for the AS men as a whole, suggesting that, although alcohol may aid social interaction, it can also be difficult to control and seriously damaging to health and relationships:

> Alcohol gave me freedom from fear of the unknown. Fear of rejection, fear of saying the wrong thing tied my tongue and kept me away from women. I didn't have a clue what to say or what might happen. Alcohol freed my tongue so that the information that I had stored in my head along with some wit, made me more attractive to women. I lost the fear, which enabled me to become a totally different person. It made my mind work much more quickly (contrary to the usual stereo-type of alcohol users) and make quick connections, so that I felt two steps ahead of most people, a facility which I have lost now that I am sober. Instead of using the normal mental pathways to solve problems, consider possibilities and see the future, alcohol seemed to open up new possibilities for me, which enabled my marriages, career and general life-style. I dared more, for I feared no consequences, and built a wholly different life from that which I would have had as a sober person. (AS male, recovering alcoholic)

> I drink. It makes it MUCH easier to socialise, but I have to restrict my intake because I come from a family of alcoholics. (AS male)

If I am out with a group of co-workers or peers, then I drink alcohol or otherwise I sit there and do not talk. (AS male)

For others, the opposite was true:

My sobriety is what sets me apart from people who could be my friends. I have reluctantly been to *a* bar, and *a* club, and *a* party. In each event, all I could see was a horde of drunken idiot assholes wasting time and money. (AS male)

3

Love and Intimacy

A sexual relationship is not always just about the physical elements. There is often a desire for emotional closeness and intimacy – the opportunity to share something special with another person. Sex without this attachment is discussed in a later chapter. Understanding and responding to the emotional requirements of a partner can be problematic for someone with Asperger Syndrome (AS), because they may simply have no clue as to what these needs are and how to meet them. 'Intimacy can be a vague concept for many individuals with AS' (Hénault 2006, p.90). They may struggle to respond to their own emotional needs. Unfortunately, there may be an expectation from a partner that they will somehow 'know' what is required emotionally, and not doing so can cause distress and confusion for both parties:

> How can a man expect to understand women if he can't even understand himself? (AS male)

Emotional support and managing feelings

Those with AS are said to have a less developed 'Theory of Mind' compared to their same age peers (Baron-Cohen 2003). This is an ability that develops in small children who, as they grow, begin to realise that they are not the only people in the world, and that others have different thoughts and knowledge from their own. Many adults with AS can find it very difficult to anticipate and comprehend that a partner may have different emotional needs. Many AS people express bewilderment at the emotional reactions of their neuro-typical (NT) partners. They may choose to do nothing in response to emotional outbursts rather than risk doing the wrong thing and unwittingly upsetting their partner further. Often the 'doing nothing' is exactly what makes things worse because this can be perceived as uncaring and cold to an NT partner. Doing something is usually better than doing nothing. Often a touch or a hug is required – quite the opposite of what some with AS prefer at times of distress. Asking your partner what they would like from you, and gently reminding them that you do not know what to do and cannot guess, may help. Emotional differences are often a common area of difficulty for AS/NT couples. This is extraordinarily hard for some people with AS to grasp because the very nature of the condition renders it impossible to see another's viewpoint; so how can you be *expected* to see another's viewpoint?

> I want to take the individuals involved in my discomfort and make them 'see' things as I do…I need to realise that other people have their own mind and their own way of doing things… But knowing this academically and being able to put it into practice are two different things. (AS female)

> When a partner doesn't agree with me on something, I feel intensely embarrassed, like I have totally misread them, and this can also lead to suppressed anger which would often come out after I had been drinking. I would look at them feeling happy/sad, and feel no emotional connection with them at all, unless their feeling coincided with mine. Only now am I learning that someone else's feeling and opinions can be as valid as my own (although it galls me to write this!). (AS male)

> I can find it hard to sympathise with a partner who is upset. It makes me angry, like they are deliberately manipulating my feelings, even though logically I know they are not. I feel like saying 'Fuck off and deal with it'! What a lovely chap I can be sometimes. (AS male)

> I don't like getting close to other people. I can't read their
> emotional cues and so they always get pissed off with me for
> something or other. (AS male)

Simon Baron-Cohen sees reduced empathising skills as being a key indicator in recognising autistic behaviour in individuals. His work on the 'extreme male brain' (Baron-Cohen 2003) states that those with AS, who are less able empathisers, are superior to the NT population in their systemising skills: seeing the world as a series of systems which operate on an action–reaction basis, logic and scientific principles.

He explains that the person with AS is engaged in a constant attempt to rationalise and systemise – to establish a number of unbreakable 'rules' by which to order their world. Unfortunately, people cannot be systemised as their reactions and behaviour are never exactly the same twice, and so no 'laws' can be established to predict that any given action will cause a known reaction. This is what causes a lot of stress for many AS people as they struggle to live in a world which is infinitely changeable and unknown.

Realising that people are irrational, unpredictable and illogical, and using that as a basis for how to deal with them, can be helpful in managing unrealistic expectations of the behaviour of others. NT people are motivated by people, flexibility and emotions, and make decisions based on these rather than logic. This makes life very complicated but simply has to be worked with as it is not going to change. There is no suggestion of rightness or wrongness in either view, but a need to recognise the differences of others and find ways to work with them to meet our own needs and objectives. Refusing to compromise with another's needs may mean that they choose not to share their time with you.

It is important to many people that their feelings are respected, even if they are different from your own. Telling a partner or friend that they are stupid for getting upset over a sad film they have seen, for example, will not make them feel safe and accepted. They may even feel that you are cruel and unkind. You may feel that you are simply expressing your opinion and find it silly to get upset over something that isn't real. It is better to provide a hug, a tissue or a cup of tea (whatever is appropriate to your relationship and if you don't know – ask) and allow your partner to have their own feelings. You would be equally unhappy if someone were to dismiss your feelings about something that was important to you and not to them. Trying to consider how you might feel when you are upset may help you to learn to consider the feelings of others.

It is also useful to note that often a person may react in similar ways to a range of situations, whether happy or sad, and may prefer a very set number of reactions from you. They may always want to be hugged when they are sad or listened to quietly (without your making any suggestions on how to fix the situation), for example. Once you have learned what their particular preference is, it is easy to do the right thing when the situation arises.

To state that those with AS lack emotions would be unjust, because many feel intense emotional reactions to things which mean something to them, when on other occasions nothing is felt or displayed (Lawson 2005). Where many NT people find support and communication a requirement at times of emotional distress, someone with AS may prefer to retreat and be alone. Being comforted may be a restorative for one person, but not for another. Understanding the different needs of individuals is important in learning the best ways to provide what is needed, which may be different from one's own needs.

Most sexual problems within relationships are the result of emotional difficulties, not physical ones. Even many physical issues have their roots within the emotional and psychological sphere. If a person is not emotionally supported, they will feel less willing to be close to their partner. If someone insists on sexual activities focusing on their own needs and interests, or disregards the emotional or sexual needs of their partner, then it is natural that the partner will eventually become resentful and perhaps decide not to engage sexually at all. It may be that a lack of understanding of AS and a perceived lack of care and emotional support from the AS partner results in a withdrawal from intimacy by one or both partners.

It is useful to learn that, particularly for NT women, practical support and intimacy can be as necessary to being receptive to sexual advances as traditional foreplay. For those with AS, particularly men, talking about emotions may be uncomfortable and unwelcome. Discussions around these issues should ideally be carried out with a spirit of wanting to reach a mutually satisfactory outcome, not one in which one party 'gets their own way' or refuses to meet a partner's need because the partner won't meet theirs. This can become a battle of wills and cause further rifts and resentment (and less sex!):

> Listening to another person talk about who they are, what they like and want from us is a vital aspect in any relationship. The difficulty for us though is that we might not find this interesting. Even though we are interested in the person themselves, listening to them talk might be uninteresting. We still need to listen though. (Lawson 2005, p.65)

Central coherence refers to the connectedness and overall 'gist' of a situation. This is something that many people with AS struggle to see, and they are therefore said to have 'weak central coherence'. If a person tends to see sex as disconnected to other events of the day (Stanford 2003) or to emotional issues such as kindness, thoughtfulness and respect, they will not understand how a partner's feelings about other issues can have an impact on their desire to have sex. For them, sex is entirely separate to whether they did the washing up, resolved an outstanding emotional issue or took time to communicate and listen to their partner, but for many people it is not. Central coherence means that everything that a partner does – yesterday, today and tomorrow – all have an impact on a person's desire to spend time, be loving and have sex with them. Consequently, the more you do to support a partner in any way possible – taking out the rubbish, doing the shopping, making dinner – the more appreciative and loving they will be towards you. Try it and see!

> Relationships for me were separate compartments that I entered into with no comprehension of what they really entailed. (AS male)

Those with AS are also reported to be passive in nature (Soderstrom, Rastam and Gillberg 2002, in Attwood 2006) and therefore not directly responsible for their own feelings and experiences. Each individual chooses how to experience their world and can make changes to this experience. This is not decided by other people. It may be difficult to understand that paying compliments and supporting a partner both practically and emotionally can change how a partner behaves towards you and therefore change the experience of the relationship. Things do not have to stay exactly as they are now, unless we continue to choose that they do. Life is full of choices that we all have the power to make (although this may seem difficult and frightening). If you had never made a decision, you wouldn't be where you are now:

> It wasn't until ten years ago (I was 50) when my therapist startled me with the idea that people can make choices… I still struggle with the notion that there really can be choices regarding how life feels, and how difficult the future might be. My experience is that this is not a choice or strategy or decision, just a matter of taking some steps that seem to be possible today, with those resources that seem to be available today. Nothing can be counted on from day to day, and each day is its own struggle. (AS male)

Being a 'couple'

It can be important to establish a sense of being a couple. This can feel strange for a person who has always seen themselves as a separate entity and perhaps spent a large part of life alone. Wendy Lawson (2005) talks about being married and going off on trips without telling her husband (she would leave him a note). She found it hard to accept her role as part of a 'couple' and that she had responsibilities to her partner. Equal partnerships mean equal responsibilities: a person cannot have the benefits of someone sharing their life without giving something back. Few would choose to remain in such a relationship that was unbalanced and unfair.

Wendy explains that it is very difficult for a person who can only see their own point of view and tends to be motivated by their own interests rather than consideration for others (Lawson 2005). Thinking of the impact of any behaviour on others is often an automatic consideration for many NT people, and so self-focused behaviour can be seen as uncaring or selfish when the person with AS is unable to see things any other way.

It is suggested that the first long-term friendship is one where children learn how to behave while playing together (Attwood 2006). The relationship may be the AS partner's first friendship and will be one of discovery and finding their way. Others may have had many friendships to learn from, so the AS person may be at a serious disadvantage and need some guidance from their partner (Stanford 2003). Some couples, where one or more partners have AS, described the other as 'my best friend' and there is often a deep closeness and companionship even when the sexual relationship is infrequent or non-existent. This bond between the partners is what some of the NT women stated as the reason for their remaining in the relationship when their sexual lives were very unsatisfactory. There seems to be a sense of safety and security about an AS partner that compensates partly for difficulties in other aspects of the relationship. Encouraging this aspect of the relationship, where a person with AS can excel, can compensate for other areas that are more difficult to accomplish. Be as good a friend as you can and share as much as possible with your partner. People like to be listened to and helped in any way you can. It makes them feel special and liked.

Having difficulties with social behaviour as a person with AS means that understanding what is expected as a partner is often very confusing. There are expectations that the AS person will 'know' what is required emotionally by having read the 'signals' and having learned throughout life as to what it means to be part of a couple. Many people with AS have lacked this external input and observation of 'what other people do' and so it all remains a mystery to them. The intuitive understanding of the requirements of the role of partner/husband/wife are not known and the person with AS may expect that life will carry on much as it did when they were unattached, not realising that there are 'rules' that come with any relationship or friendship. As the partner of someone with AS, it is necessary to learn and understand that this apparent lack of care is not deliberate. Many partners of AS people report feeling unloved and uncared for, and this can have long-term mental health issues (Aston 2003). This may be more to do with a lack of understanding of each partner's communication style and expression of emotion than any intent of cruelty by the AS partner. In our study, some people with AS expressed a difficulty in being emotionally close to their partner and in being able to communicate this difficulty. Those who understood that their partner with AS was doing the best they could were able to have happy and appreciative relationships together:

I asked my husband (AS) to please be nice to me. He looked at me blankly and said: 'I have absolutely no idea how to be nice to you'. (NT female)

Even after marriage relations of 20 years or more, I still don't know the person or share in their style of trust and naturalness. (AS male)

I have found it very hard to be emotionally close to my spouse. He (AS) doesn't understand how to connect with me sometimes. It's difficult to know if he is able to truly appreciate my feelings or if he's just learned to pretend to 'get it'. (NT female)

It takes a lot for me to let others in about my emotional issues. That is the hardest part of being in a relationship with another person. (AS male)

I just have never 'connected' well. I feel there is not as much of me to share about. (AS male)

My (AS) partner is looking for a new job. He is applying for work overseas. We live in England. He knows I cannot go with him if he goes to live and work abroad but does not see that he perhaps ought to discuss this with me. He believes that our relationship will not change even if we live in different countries. He is bewildered by the idea that, as a couple, he should consider my opinions when making life-changing plans. (NT female)

The partner was often seen to be the only person required to meet all social and emotional needs by the partner with AS (Aston 2003). This may not be the case for an NT partner who may need to maintain a wider social circle in order to meet all of these needs. The AS partner should see this as beneficial to the overall harmony of the relationship and both partners should respect and acknowledge the different social and support needs of the other. Finding someone who makes a person with AS feel comfortable seems to be an important aspect of maintaining the relationship. No one should feel uncomfortable in a relationship, but it is necessary to try to accommodate the needs of both partners as much as they are compatible:

> He (AS) regards me as his only real friend and the only one he really needs to feel somewhat close to. (NT female)

> I think he (AS) feels that there's no one for him but me and that if I were to ever leave, he'd be alone and lost. (NT female)

> I don't really want to spend time with anyone else and doubt my ability to manage a relationship with anyone else anyway. She simply gets me. (AS male)

> My husband (AS) has never had another romantic relationship with anyone but me. Never kissed another person or even held hands with another person. He has had few real friendships… For the most part he seems entirely happy having me be the sole personal relationship of any sort in his life. (NT female)

Exposure anxiety and expectations

Donna Williams, a woman with autism, discusses what she terms 'exposure anxiety' in her book (Williams 2003, p.171). Donna describes how she craved closeness and yet felt compelled to shun and reject it when offered directly, perceiving anything given as an invasion. The only way that she could connect with others was indirectly, through objects and a sense of indifference. She says that it is easier to select the 'wrong people' because they may well display this calm indifference that is less threatening than being the focus of someone's attention and love.

Friendships that don't involve interacting but simply sharing space together are preferred by people who are affected by exposure anxiety. It is enough to know that the person is relaxed enough to be themselves, and it is a good sign that they are enjoying the relationship. To ask for direct feedback causes anxiety because the person is put into the spotlight:

I had a fear of closeness as I was aware that having sex with a girlfriend meant an involvement. I took it seriously as for me it was often something I felt unable to get out of – leave the relationship. I wasn't able to say no; I had a feeling I owed them something for letting me sleep with them. (AS male)

Demands and expectations

For some AS relationships, there can be issues around the NT partner craving validation and feedback that they are interesting and still valued in the relationship. This may be especially important in an AS relationship where the AS partner gives fewer neuro-typical indications of care than in NT relationships (this is a generalised statement based on previous research (Aston 2003; Attwood 2006)). Research suggests that mental health issues can arise for an NT partner in managing the less empathic and brutally honest ways of their AS partner (Aston 2003). This demand and focus of attention on the AS partner to deliver what is required can cause anxiety and confusion.

The person with AS may be aware that they are expected to fix the situation with some words or gestures, but they may have no clue as to how that is to be achieved. It may be that, in the event of not knowing what to say, they choose to say nothing at all for fear of getting it wrong and making things worse. Unfortunately, the NT partner may interpret silence as a deliberate ignoring of their feelings and be even more deeply hurt and emotionally demanding, causing more anxiety for and silence from the AS partner. This is not the fault of the person with AS, but a difference in communication styles and understanding. Finding a way to tell your partner how you care about them may help them to see evidence of your feelings in a way that you can manage easily and regularly. Some people need regular words or demonstrations of love, and believe that you no longer love them if you don't show or say it. This can happen quite quickly for some people. They require frequent top-ups of affection and love.

For some people, the fact that other people have expectations of them can be stressful. By having these external expectations imposed upon them, the person with AS can feel that they are unable to live up to these demands and that they are destined to fail. This may be after having 'failed' so many times in the past because of not understanding what was required, and having developed very low self-confidence and self-belief as a result. For some, there are issues with 'being told what to do' and an automatic rejection of even reasonable requests for fear of 'getting it wrong'. The person may feel forced into an active position, rather than the more passive role that is the default state of many AS people. There may be an acute awareness that, unless the person reacts in the 'right' way, something unknown and potentially terrible will happen, although what this is and how this can be avoided is unfathomable:

> I can really relate to an inability to accept love and closeness. This often brings feelings of anger up in me, like I am losing a part of myself by accepting closeness with someone else. I long for this closeness, but when I get it, it seems that I am being 'colonised'. I get the sensation that I am losing my 'separateness' which I adore. I like visiting the rest of the human race, but as long as I do it as and when *I* want to, there is no problem. My first instinct when someone else arranges something without first consulting me is to scream and stamp my feet – then lie down and roll around until I am puce in the face. Fortunately, this rarely happens these days. (AS male)

> I suppose, like many people, it boils down to the feeling 'if you REALLY knew me, you wouldn't come within a mile of me'. That there is something unacceptable about the self that one cannot bear to be revealed. There is also the fear of losing one's autonomy – the complete freedom to please oneself without paying regard to the wishes or feelings of another. I think that alcohol enabled me to dampen these feelings down, so that I was able to live with those I loved, and get through the 'bad' times of sublimating my will by getting the false euphoria of booze. (AS male)

> He (AS) rarely shares confidences with anyone because he can't stand anyone 'telling him what to do' and he feels this way about any unsolicited advice. (NT female)

I do have difficulty with particular emotional projections, expectations and needs. (AS male)

Showing love and feelings

Being in love could be described as essentially monotropic: a single-minded, obsessive state (Lawson 2005, p.29) for anyone, which those with AS can do especially well! The person concerned may become the narrow interest of the person with AS for a while. Problems can occur if the attraction is not reciprocated and the interest does not diminish accordingly, or if the attraction is reciprocated and the interest does diminish shortly after!

The state of AS is often one of extremes: all or nothing, black and white — all features of a monotropic mind. This can result in either forming no attachments or becoming over-attached and dependent on others. Wendy Lawson talks about not being able to separate 'self' from 'other' and a lack of understanding of personal space (for self or other) (2005, p.47). Difficulties coping with life can make it easier to live through another person, rather than make decisions for yourself. This can be a big responsibility for the person who finds themselves with a passive partner, and it can be dangerous for the person with AS who may not have good judgement when deciding who to trust with their emotions. Being aware that there are subtleties between the all-or-nothing states which come so naturally can help when making decisions. Finding a trustworthy person to assist in making these choices may be vital in avoiding missing important information that you have been unable to see:

> I seem able to cope a lot better if I have a binary opinion about everything: it's either one thing or the other. I either like something or I don't, I can do something or I can't, I can see a resolution or I can't. (AS male)

> I surrender just about every decision to whoever is there. Making choices and decisions that involve an element of shared responsibility is a nightmare: because I never know what anyone else is thinking or their motivations. I can never get it right; I can't second guess. (AS male)

I have issues with emotional closeness with my husband…
About the only emotions he (AS) feels are anger and
pleasure. (NT female)

This all-or-nothing mind state also makes it difficult for some to decode
the complexities of emotions. Some people with AS find subtle emotions
hard to interpret – both in themselves and in others. Their understanding
may be confined to extremes of emotion such as joy or anger (Hénault
2006). More subtle feelings may be confusing and hard to manage or
even recognise. Some people with AS have admitted to deliberately pro-
voking extreme reactions because they are unable to 'see' more subtle
facial and bodily responses. By pushing someone to a higher state of
distress, they can appreciate what emotion is being presented. This trait
can also result in the relationship being seen as 'perfect' or 'unbearable',
veering from one extreme to the other with great speed. The partner can
feel as though they are walking a fine line to keep things settled and calm
within the relationship. A sense of 'walking on eggshells' has been
described by NT partners who can be unwilling to express their own
emotions for fear of the fallout from doing so. Just the mention of a minor
dissatisfaction may send the AS partner into deep despair or indignant
dispute. Some NT partners simply don't have the energy for arguing and
so keep their true feelings to themselves. This can have a damaging effect
on the relationship in the long term because resentment and contempt
can arise. It is important to be honest and admit when you are confused or
cannot read the emotional signals from others. Partners also need to learn
to state clearly what they are feeling, rather than expect you to guess.

For some with AS, emotions are simply overwhelming, nameless
physical sensations, which are to be avoided or subdued, and this can be
hard for both partners to live with – one feeling too much, the other
seeing little evidence of emotion from their partner and feeling unloved.
This can be the case for NT partners who do not understand how different the AS perspective can be. It is sometimes useful to state that you
don't know what is expected, so that your partner does not assume that
you are deliberately ignoring or choosing not to support them. Other
issues can also be present, which prevent some people with AS from
feeling comfortable in becoming emotionally close to another person.
Low self-esteem, difficulty in reading signals, language communication

differences and exposure to the expectations and demands of another person can all cause anxiety:

> Anxiety issues, as well as lack of experience, make the expression of emotions difficult and impede the process of reaching any significant degree of emotional closeness. (AS male)

For some people with AS, sex and physical affection can be the easiest way to express how they feel about a partner without the need for words (Aston 2003). It can be a tangible, physical way of showing love, and some partners of those with AS report an intensity and intimacy in love-making that they have not experienced with fellow NT partners. This physical connection is important for those who are unable to verbally articulate their strong feelings for their partner, although the partner may not realise that this is a demonstration of love and misinterpret requests for sex as purely physical. Just as a partner with AS may be good at showing love in practical, concrete ways rather than romantic gestures, sex may be the ultimate physical representation of emotional connection. Telling a partner that this is your way of showing love may help in their appreciating this as a sign instead of using words.

It can sometimes be reported that those with AS are incapable of forming emotional bonds with others, and that they are cold and harsh. As an AS trainer, the author has heard: 'They don't have any emotions' said regularly from delegates as a commonly held belief about those with autism/AS. This is completely untrue. It is typical for the NT population to measure emotional capacity by physical presentation because that is the norm; because an individual may not engage in social smiling, eye contact and displays of emotion on a regular basis, it may be assumed that these feelings don't exist. A shift in perception is required to understand the different demonstrations of attachment in those with AS.

Some partners with AS who responded to the questionnaire were extremely physically and emotionally affectionate, and this was enjoyed by many partners and understood as a non-verbal indication of their love. Others may perceive this need and display of affection to be overwhelm-ing and unwelcome (Attwood 2006). This was not identified in this study except when the constant physical contact was overtly sexual in nature:

I believe that for a happy life, emotional closeness with at least one other person is a necessity. I may desire more emotional closeness than normal people desire. (AS male)

To feel close to me, he (AS) wants to have sex every single day and does not see why I need that emotional type of closeness. (NT female)

I don't have an issue getting emotionally close to anyone, in fact I think I've overwhelmed some men with the emotions I do show. (AS female)

He (AS) really likes to touch all the time. He doesn't want sexual touch very much…but he likes to have small physical contact going on all the time we are together… It has always seemed like the touch is a way of making sure I'm still there. (NT female)

He (AS) is so loving and affectionate. He will kiss my hair or face at every opportunity. I never tire of this gentle, wonderful attention. It lets me know he is happy, relaxed and OK. (NT female)

I don't always know how much is enough. I am very conscious of giving too much and they either get scared off or get an inaccurate picture of what I feel. (AS male)

He touches me in a playfully sexual manner all the time. It makes me laugh and I love it. It shows he is comfortable with me, which I know has been a rare occurrence for him. (NT female)

I cuddle with them and let them hug me. I spend time with them; I like to have them near me even when I need quiet time. Sometimes I tell them (that I love them) but sometimes I have trouble with those words. (AS female)

Because of my husband's AS it is often hard for him to express these things to me and I often feel it is unfair of me to ask. I become concerned he'll misinterpret and think I'm

> saying he's failing me instead of hearing me ask for reassur-
> ance. (NT female)

Those with AS form strong attachments to other people in the same way
as anyone else, and these can be far more logically based than with NT
people and less easily broken. A person with AS may begin or remain in a
relationship because it has very clear benefits to them or, more impor-
tantly perhaps, there is an absence of negative stress. Anyone who raises
stress levels will be an unlikely candidate for a relationship. Although
there is an element of these practical needs being met in NT relationships,
it is more likely to be an emotionally motivated decision, rather than a
practical one. There is also perhaps less willingness to admit this practical
bias for some NT people who claim their relationship is based on 'chemistry' but who may not experience the same chemistry were their partner
to be less financially able, have poor fashion sense or be politically
opposed to them. This is seen to be somewhat 'unromantic' and is sometimes viewed distastefully even though, I propose, it is part of most
people's decision as to whom to be with. It is not as honestly stated as by
those with AS.

Many people with AS maintain that the greatest sign of their love for
a partner is their continued presence, and they don't easily understand
the need for reassurance and verbal demonstrations. 'I'm here, aren't I?' is
a genuine reaction to the question: 'Do you still love me?' If they didn't,
they wouldn't be – simple as that.

Wendy Lawson describes the care of love as 'wanting to be with and
wanting to do good for'. She states that the 'attractively presented
emotion' that accompanies the non-AS version of love is 'just extraneous:
it's not the core' (Lawson 2005, p.29). Ultimately, non-AS people also
choose relationships based on benefit/pay-off, but may hide this under a
veil of emotion:

> For most of my life I didn't realise what the word intimacy
> means; now I have learned, I have to admit it sounds most
> unpleasant and unnatural. Desirable emotional close-
> ness…is for me based on politeness, respectable language
> and mutual respect. (AS male)

I once thought I was incapable of falling in love with someone and connecting the way that others seemed to. My partners were chosen at random. Just in the past two years I have learned that I am capable of forming a connection. Curiously enough this connection is with another individual who has AS. I wonder if that is part of what made it possible. (AS female)

One of [the] things that caused me the most discomfort and difficulty in my past relationships was my 'over-attachment' to individuals of the same sex. (AS female)

The demonstrations of love from an AS partner may be more practical than romantic in the traditional sense, and may further indicate the independent path that the person with AS chooses to take in life. As mentioned previously, the person with AS may have the emotional maturity of a much younger person (Attwood 2006) and a tendency to experience and examine emotions intellectually rather than 'feeling' them as the organic sensation described by NT individuals. This can mean that their emotional responses can sound quite scientific and logical rather than a spontaneous burst of emotion, although some people report great eloquence and romance from their partners, sometimes in the form of poetry, written words or cards, rather than in spoken words:

Meaningless gestures and dead plants are not appropriate signs of my love. For me, being here, in this relationship, is the best indication and measure of my feelings for _____. I don't see why I should adhere to society's expectations as to how I demonstrate my feelings. (AS male)

The marriage counsellor asked him why he (AS) loved me. He said: 'Because she's clever, organised and good at filling in forms.' (NT female)

Changing the oil in the car, taking out the rubbish or doing the washing-up may be easier than saying 'I love you' for an AS partner. They may feel that providing for the family is enough of an indication of care. An NT partner may feel the need to say it several times a day and expect it to be reciprocated. Neither is wrong, but a lack of awareness of these differences can cause major problems. Recognising and appreciating these different needs is important for the relationship. Sometimes it is necessary to ask for signs of love because the AS person may not know that they are required. For an NT person, this can feel as though there is no spontaneity or romance if they have to ask, but without asking it is unlikely to happen. For the AS person, asking for guidance on how to help and support a partner may be greatly appreciated and is better than doing nothing at all or waiting for a request to be made:

> I am aware my love showing tends to be more in practical ways than verbally. (AS male)

> I fake it in order to keep her happy. (AS male)

> I would show that I think of her every day. I would treat her to 'the little things that count' like occasional chocolate or flowers or whatever she prefers, just for the sake of being nice. (AS male)

> My presence, my politeness, my kindness and tolerance would be the major ways I'd show love. (AS male)

For some AS men who had been in relationships that had ended, there was a sense of remorse that they had not done enough to demonstrate their love for their partners or had not really known what was required of them. Some of the NT women, who were no longer in relationships with their AS partners, expressed some bitterness about the perceived lack of attention and care from their former partners. Usually, the presence of AS was not known until long into the relationship, by which time it may have been too late for some couples to reframe their interactions with each other to include new mutual understanding:

> I never thought about it (showing love). I just loved her. I didn't know that showing was an issue. I thought you just needed to love. I now am aware that I was mistaken. (AS male)

> I'm not the slightest bit content with the amount of love and appreciation that I showed my partners precisely because I can see that it didn't work. Another reason I wouldn't want

to have a partner any more. I wouldn't want to be inadequate any more. (AS male)

My wife is prone to say she doesn't really know me, every now and then. (AS male)

After the experience of my married life thus far, I will never inflict someone else with me again. (AS male)

After 13 years in the relationship, I still know almost nothing of my wife. (AS male)

I was incredibly greedy for love and understanding. Part of me believes that there is no love in the universe, anywhere. Even when I'm being showered with love it runs off into the gutter and is lost in moments. (AS male)

Many NT women questioned did not feel loved by their partners and felt that they were not appreciated or cared for by them. Self-esteem is often low in those with AS and some may give up trying to do the right thing for their partner because they believe they will always fail (Aston 2003). Failure is often very difficult to bear for those with AS. These feelings of unmet need lead to resentment, which is damaging to the relationship and will eventually lead to its breakdown, or else depression and contempt. Knowledge of AS and its effects on a person is necessary for both partners to understand that neither partner is deliberately harming the other, and to increase awareness of the different ways in which each partner communicates. Both partners need to remember why they are in the relationship and make efforts to show love to their partners (and find out how to if they don't know) even if they don't feel like it (it can be especially important to do it at these times) and to recognise each other's way of demonstrating love because it is sure to be different from their own. Little and often is a good start:

I say he (AS) blocks me out and won't let me in and he says I know him more than anyone on earth. What we want just doesn't meet. The middle ground doesn't reach! (NT female)

Those who were appreciative of their AS partner's efforts showed a tenderness and pleasure from their interactions. They seemed to understand their partner's difficulty in expressing themselves and made adjustments to their own behaviour in order to relieve the pressure on their partner. The AS women (all of whom had AS partners) demonstrated a greater contentment in their relationships, perhaps due to a similar understanding of AS needs. They were able to recognise the ways in which their partner did express feelings and care, even when these were quite different from what they would have preferred. This resulted in a more content and unstressed AS partner, which in turn benefited the relationship as a whole. One partner changing their approach can have a big impact:

> I touch him in reassuring ways throughout our day and when I see a certain look come across his face I ask if he needs a hug. (NT female)

> I ask him what he needs and tell him it's OK to let me know in any way he can. (NT female)

> He's (AS) not one for typical romantic stuff, but he'll do other, more practical things: clean out my car or draw me a huge detailed map of (city) from scratch on the computer. If I ask him for something…he'll make himself obsessed with making me happy on that issue; change habits and generally go out of his way to study, understand and provide every aspect of what I've asked. (NT female)

> Be there for him (AS), talk to him when he wants to talk. Leave him alone when he wants to be left alone. Hug him. Kiss him. (AS female)

> (I show him I love him) a million different ways; everything from doing little things for him to telling him, to physical affection. (NT female)

> It was awkward at first for me to pick up on his (AS) ways of expressing love for me, but now that I get it, it's become almost preferred because it's so genuine and without pretence. (NT female)

Sometimes he (AS) expresses love by simply cackling like a madman when I tell him I love him. (NT female)

He (AS) is not good at Christmas, Valentine's Day or on my birthday but when he feels not obligated to do something is when he will go out and buy me something. (NT female)

4

Sensory Perception and Solitude

Although not part of the diagnostic criteria, it is a widely held belief, validated by numerous personal accounts, that many individuals with Asperger Syndrome (AS) and autism experience differences in sensory perception. Some anecdotal reports suggest that all those with AS are affected in some way. The results of this questionnaire show that to be the case with over 80 per cent of those with AS reporting some sensitivity – either positive or negative – in at least one of the senses.

One sense may be hypersensitive to compensate for a lack of sensitivity in another (Hénault 2006). For some people, this aspect of their AS is more difficult to manage than social issues (Attwood 2006). The effects of sensory differences can manifest as an over- or under-sensitivity to any of the physical senses and, to add to the confusion, these effects can vary from day to day, from situation to situation. One day a certain noise may be tolerable, on another day the same sound will be unbearably painful. There may be a mix-up of sensory responses called synaesthesia, where a person may experience one sense by a sensation in another; some may experience taste as a visual sense, describing the sensation of food as a colour rather than as a sensation of the tongue (a taste). This may explain why some individuals with AS dislike certain colours of food as they may know they don't like something purely by the visual sensation it produces.

The degree and particular sensory crossover differs in all individuals and is an example of the hypersensory perception some with AS enjoy or endure that the majority struggle to perceive. There may be vestibular (balance) differences, which result in the person feeling unstable unless they are rocking or swinging their arms. There may be proprioception differences, which are manifested by stretch receptors in the muscles and sensory neurons within the inner ear. These senses allow us to know where parts of our body are without looking at them: the 'sense' of the body, being able to walk in the dark or put a finger on our nose with our eyes closed.

Many of these sensations are often unnoticeable to most neurotypical (NT) people, who are unable to comprehend the extremity of the reaction of the AS person. In fact, there may be a refusal to believe that someone is physically incapable of tolerating a texture or smell that most people have no problem with. It requires a shift in perception to trust that the person with AS's reality is often substantially different.

Some of the physical manifestations of sensory sensitivity may look unusual to the onlooker and appear strange when first meeting someone: rocking, swaying, facial and vocal tics may be apparent. Some individuals will sniff or lick anything new that they come into contact with, or react adversely to anyone wearing certain fabrics or scents. It is simply another way of identifying objects and people that enter the individual's environment. This can be difficult for someone to accommodate if they are unaware of the cause of the reaction.

It is important that the AS partner communicates what sensory experiences they are having because these will be individual to them and not known to others. Care needs to be taken when trying to stop these behaviours or reacting negatively to them because they clearly perform a function or they wouldn't exist. If the behaviour is seen to be socially unacceptable, the behaviour may have adverse consequences and cause others to react negatively. Some people with AS are completely unaware that this is the case and do not realise why they are socially avoided. It can be enlightening for the person to understand the cause of some of their social difficulties.

Of course, after learning of the potential consequences, you may choose to continue the behaviour, but others do not have to tolerate it. It may be necessary to agree a compromise on when and how often you engage in your sensory enjoyment, depending on the level of impact it has on others. If your sensory enjoyment involves sniffing your partner's feet, then it requires their compliance and agreement. If you only require to sniff your own feet, then there is more scope for meeting your own needs, although you may still need to compromise by only doing this privately.

One AS man enjoyed cracking his joints on a regular basis in any public situation, much to the annoyance and discomfort of all around him. Despite seeing the reactions of others and being asked not to do it by many people, he was unable to understand how a simple noise could cause such a strong reaction and saw it as a problem for the individuals concerned and not for him. His partner explained to him that his behaviour may have longer-term consequences because others will remember that he not only made this horrible noise, but also showed no concern for their feelings. This in turn may mean that he is not invited to social occasions and is perceived as rude. He was able to grasp this concept intellectually, but still derives too much pleasure from cracking his joints to stop. His partner has to put up with feeling uncomfortable when he does it.

The overall effect of too much information and sensory input coming at a person with AS is known as 'sensory overload': the point where it is all too much and the person needs to shut down in some way, either by retreating or becoming highly agitated, angry or anxious. This is a real and overwhelming experience for the individual and should be taken as a sign that they need to be removed from the situation. This can seem hard to believe for a person who does not become overloaded by the normal environment or affected by ordinary, everyday sounds, textures and odours, but it certainly does exist for many people with AS. There is often a greater need for withdrawal and solitude for those with AS. This is in effect a shutting-down time during which the demands of everyday life can be switched off. Solitude is a great restorative for those with AS in a way that it appears not to be for NT people, who may prefer to be around people when they are relaxing.

Within a personal relationship, the effects of feeling discomfort through the senses can cause distress for both parties. Certain activities and situations may be avoided by the AS partner, leaving their partner feeling rejected without knowing why. An AS partner's complete withdrawal can also be taken personally as a need to escape or avoid the partner. This is a truth: there is a need to withdraw, but from all humanity and social contact, not personally and specifically from the partner. There is a distinct difference.

The main senses that have been reported as important in intimate relationships are those of sensitivity to smell, touch and the feel of specific textures (Aston 2003), although noise and general overload can also cause issues. This heightened sensory perception can also result in an intense pleasure and calm elicited from a variety of sensory stimuli, to an extent that NT individuals generally do not experience. Some people with AS express pity for NT people whose sensory perception is less finely tuned and who fail to register or notice many of the joys of the sensory world. This is the plus side of different sensory perception, where a person can be absorbed and transfixed by light playing on a wall, the scent of new plastic or the sensation of touching soft, smooth skin. Some individuals describe near orgasmic states of delight when ensconced in their favourite sensory activities and can be occupied for hours in doing them. Engaging in these activities is important to maintain low stress levels, but they may need to be limited if sharing time with a partner. A fine balance needs to be achieved in maintaining your own well-being and attending to the needs of a partner, should you choose to have one. Only you can decide what is most important to you.

Noise

Some individuals are highly sensitive to specific noises, frequencies or volume of sound. Over 25 per cent of those with AS who answered the question said that noise was an issue for them, in relation to sex. This was an entirely negative experience for those concerned, unlike some of the other sensory differences. They were unable to filter out these unwanted distractions and unable to focus on anything or anyone while they were occurring. While a person without AS may be able to ignore background noise, an AS person is less likely to be able to do so. This may mean that the person is unable to engage intimately or perform sexually as their stress level may rise due to the noise. For a partner, this may be seen as a rejection and an excuse for the AS partner to avoid intimacy. This will generally not be the case and will be a genuine cause of discomfort. For others, sounds can be calming or even stimulating:

> When he (AS) hears a noise at a certain pitch he will clamp
> his hands over his ears and keep them there, wherever we

are, whatever we are doing. This gives him the appearance of a small child even though he is over six feet tall and a grown man. (NT female)

(I) generally don't like the idea of other people being nearby or in the same house – privacy thing – any distractions not good. (AS male)

(He) (AS) often hears things that no one else can hear, like a monitor buzzing or a phone charger making a high-pitched noise. These sounds drive him nuts and he can't stay in the same room as them. (NT female)

I am unfortunately sensitive to the sounds of repetitive squeaking sounds, primarily those emitted from a squeaky bed being sexed upon. This is more of a learned response rather than an inherent quality with my perceptions. (AS male)

Smell

There may be an intense enjoyment or stimulation from certain odours and/or a strong dislike or physical intolerance to other smells. This needs to be communicated sensitively to a partner because it can be hard for someone to hear that their natural scent may be intolerable. This can feel embarrassing and rejecting and be taken very personally and offensively. Twenty-five per cent of those with AS in our study reported being sensitive to odours and smells. Some people articulated a great pleasure from perfumes or natural bodily smells, whereas others were unable to tolerate certain smells, whether chemical or naturally occurring:

I don't always like the odour of body fluids. (AS male)

My spouse (AS) does not like anything with fragrance, so I use unscented everything. (NT female)

I love the smells, sweat, wetness, nakedness etc. (AS male)

I do love certain perfumes – I find *L'Air du Temps* incredibly arousing. (AS male)

Could never come close to a smoker or drinker. (AS male)

Smell – love it. (AS male)

I do not like any kind of bodily fragrances – perfume, cologne, scented deodorant etc. – things I call 'artificial pheromones'. With people, the best smell is no smell at all. (AS male)

Smells are very important in my love life. They can really enhance it. (AS male)

Touch

The physical contact of a partner is a major part of most personal relationships. To be able to receive and give loving touch is deeply intimate and special to most people. This comfort that is felt from touch from another person is not always experienced in the same way by a person with AS who has sensitivity in this area. The most commonly reported sensory issue was that of touch with almost 60 per cent of those with AS saying that they experienced an intense desire and enjoyment of certain types of touch, or alternatively an inability to tolerate close physical contact. Some partners said how distressed and upset they had felt when their partners pulled away immediately after sex because the closeness had become overwhelming for them. It is necessary to communicate these feelings and find a solution that will meet the needs of both partners.

Certain types of touch – light or deep – may be perceived as unpleasant and even painful. This is very unusual in NT people, most of whom have less specific requirements as to intensity of touch. The inability to tolerate physical contact can also cause sadness and depression for both partners (Hénault 2006). Unexpected touch, such as being hugged or having an arm put around one, can be very distressing and provoke anxiety and even anger. One man with AS said that he felt like punching his girlfriends in the face when they put an arm around him unexpectedly. He felt restricted by their touch. He also explained that the level of touch from another was never quite the right intensity – either too heavy or too light. He enjoyed physical closeness when he was in control of the contact: when he was doing the holding and hugging. It can be perceived as an invasion to touch a person without their consent. For him this is an aspect of AS that is about the need for controlling situations in order to ensure their predictability. A person with AS may be quite comfortable if they are initiating the touch but go rigid if they are touched by someone else. This situation will then become unpredictable and unknown and provoke anxiety.

Some people have desensitised themselves in order to be able to tolerate touch by increasing their exposure to different forms of contact in small measures until they can manage to tolerate it to a reasonable extent. Knowing how and when a person will be touched can help. The element of surprise and not being prepared or in control can affect some people's ability to cope with being touched or embraced. Asking people to warn you in advance or ask your permission before they are about to touch you may help to alleviate some of the uncomfortable feelings. Alternatively, politely ask people not to touch you, but understand that this will be difficult within intimate personal relationships because it is a generally expected facet.

There may be sensitivity to certain fabrics and, if a partner is wearing these textures, they cannot be touched. The person may not be aware that this is why they feel discomfort if they do not have a great sense of self-awareness, and it may take observation over a period of time to identify what the triggers are for avoiding contact. Bedclothes, washing powders and anything that alters the feel of something may be unbearable:

> When I 'broke down' my wife would want to hold me and that was the last thing I wanted. (AS male)

> I do not like light touch. Light touch almost hurts. (AS female)

> I do not enjoy much kissing or too much touching around my head or neck. (AS male)

> I do like a full body hug. (AS male)

> I am more aroused when both my partner and I are totally naked. (AS male)

I found some of the most arousing stimulation I have had is to be kissed on my back, and also to have words written on my back – used to play this game with a partner where we had to guess what was being written by our fingertips. (AS male)

Don't like touch in certain places (e.g. stomach, lower back, neck). (AS male)

Touch is overwhelming, it is OK while having sex or cuddling, but is very distracting otherwise. Like when trying to sleep. (AS male)

I guess I didn't like being touched or held as it was a similar feeling to wearing jewellery or watches, being encumbered and not totally free and separate. I used to joke with my exes 'no PDAs!' (public displays of affection) such as hand-holding or arms around waist. It felt like I was wearing clothes one size too small – I preferred the sense of freedom and liberation being totally free gave me. (AS male)

Delicate touch is OK, firm touch is OK, somewhere in the middle is tickly and annoying. (AS male)

Even hugging him (AS) has to be short and you have to stop when you have just begun. He gets claustrophobic if things are too tight or too close. Whenever we touch it can't be too light or too hard. There is not much which is right and it is a bit of an art which I haven't mastered. (NT female)

I don't like someone trying to hold me. I'll kiss her but only because she wants me to. (AS male)

I like to hold her close after sex, sometimes with a few moments of rocking. (AS male)

I enjoy feeling his body with my eyes closed. I get more sensory input and understand his body better that way. (AS female)

I have a preference for smoothness and hairlessness in myself and my partners. This is not inspired by a desire for femininity; it's just me. (AS male)

He's (AS) also hypersensitive to touch after climax and I have to be careful to let him 'dismount' painlessly and to initiate all movement and touching after sex. (NT female)

He (AS) hates light touch... He won't kiss me any more. This is my biggest issue with our sex life. Without kissing it feels 'cold' to me. (NT female)

Sexual intercourse may cause pain for some hypersensitive individuals – for women this may be vaginal pain and for men this may mean quick ejaculation or discomfort. The opposite effect of hypo- or undersensitivity may mean that some people require extreme stimulation in order to feel anything which arouses. Masturbation may be preferred in these cases as the speed and firmness can be controlled to the intensity required for orgasm more effectively than penetration (Hénault 2006). A lack of sensitivity to touch can mean that certain activities are preferred:

I can only orgasm through penetration with a partner. No other stimulation is anywhere near as pleasurable. I am not particularly sensitive so I need more friction to achieve orgasm. I have never had an orgasm orally or manually with a partner. (AS male)

I like rougher stimulation. I like my neck to be sucked. I like to be bit. I like to be slapped. (AS female)

I am a masochist so I do enjoy pain and it does make sex more enjoyable for me. (AS female)

I prefer a firm touch. I like to be held tightly and sometimes bound. (AS female)

Masturbation and physical pumping of his (AS) penis increases during periods of stress. Sometimes he will need to have pressure on his penis for hours. (NT female)

Aesthetics/visual

For some, visual imagery is very important as a means of enjoying the sights before their eyes. For others, it can detract from the enjoyment of another's body in an intimate situation. The difficulty in maintaining eye contact or visual gaze can be problematic within intimate situations as 'gazing into one another's eyes' is seen as required for 'connecting'. The lack of eye contact in love-making can be distressing for an NT partner who may perceive that the partner is not really 'there' if they are avoiding their gaze. Eye contact in this context is extremely important for some partners. Finding a way to manage this may require communication or some de-sensitising to enable you to do this for brief periods.

> An ageing or diseased body would always put me off, regardless of how good my relationship with the person might be… I can't come close to a partner with any real defects. The human body itself I can only cope with by 'distancing' myself from it mentally. I don't like the nitty gritty contact with the other's body. (AS male)

> I look at a woman's body somewhat unrealistically and non-physically. I shut out the actual physicality of the body. (AS male, as above)

> Very visual, greatly enjoy being able to see what is going on. (AS male)

> I do enjoy seeing him enjoy what I am doing. (AS female)

> My happiest and most innocent and childlike sort of sex was a bit like playing and replaying a game of 'you show me yours and I'll show you mine'. I guess that my sexuality is very visually centred like an unbelieving adolescent. (AS male)

Overload and need for solitude

It seems to be the case that many people with AS become overloaded with the demands of everyday life and people, due to the extra effort involved in navigating the confusing world with unreadable communications and unknown expectations. It is not surprising, then, that the need to 'switch off' or escape from even those closest to a person can arise with regularity. Without these opportunities for retreat, a person with AS can become depressed, withdrawn or angry as they struggle to cope with continued demands for conversation and intimacy. The desire for sex may decline for those under this kind of daily pressure. The person with AS may assume that everyone finds the same restorative effect from solitude and not understand why their withdrawal is met with such resistance. They may not understand that for many NT people withdrawal equates to abandonment, rejection and punishment. It is important to communicate the benefits of and need for solitude to close friends and partners so that they will accommodate your need to be alone.

> I'm aware of how difficult it is to handle the need for withdrawal and personal space within a same-house same-bed relationship. It won't prevent me from attempting this again, though. (AS male)

> I like being totally alone in the routine of daily living. Alone at night before bed, on getting up in the morning… I like female company for compartmentalised recreation only. (AS male)

> Sometimes I feel myself distancing even with my partner, whom I love dearly. It's almost like my emotions need a rest. (AS male)

> Sometimes I feel like I have to get away, just to have some time on my own for a few hours. (AS male)

> My husband (AS) is not afraid of being alone, in fact he needs some time alone. (NT female)

Hygiene

For some partners, cleanliness can be an issue. This can manifest itself in different ways. Some partners of those with AS complain that their partner has no sense of personal hygiene and has to be reminded to shower and clean themselves before expecting sex. Ensuring your own cleanliness is a sign of respect for a partner and some partners will legitimately refuse to have sex if their partner has not washed recently. Not only will they be upset at their partner being dirty, but they will also be hurt by the apparent lack of care and concern for them by showing up unwashed. This is a small but vital effort that can improve relations between partners:

> My partner (AS) would not always be aware that he should be clean before attempting sex. I found this upsetting that he didn't make this effort before becoming intimate with my body. (NT female)

> I have a vivid sense of smell and sometimes my Aspie husband is a 'pig' – does not shower for four days straight...sits around the house passing gas loudly...and these things make me want to run the other way rather than have sex. (NT female)

Typically, in the all-or-nothing, black and white AS world, the other issue can be the opposite scenario, where the AS partner will insist on fastidious cleanliness from their partner and sometimes display an aversion to the bodily fluids that result from sexual stimulation. If the person with AS expresses this too distastefully, it can cause upset for the partner who may want to enjoy the intimacy of the moment. Finding an acceptable compromise and communicating how it feels will help this:

> He (AS) used to leap up immediately after sex to clean himself. It made me feel as though I had contaminated him. I just wanted to be held by him, not be thrown a tissue to clean myself. (NT female)

> He (AS) doesn't like to be sticky or to have any oil or lubrication used on him. (NT female)

> He (AS) wanted to experiment with oral sex but would stop in the middle of necking to ask me to take a shower (even if I had one just before going to see him) so he could give a go at oral sex. (NT female)

It can be difficult to understand the reality of the AS partner's inability to tolerate heightened enjoyment of specific sensory sensations. Clear communication from both partners will help to minimise any distress or confusion relating to these differences. Both partners need to express their thoughts and feelings and listen to the reality of the other person. Just because it is not one partner's experience does not mean it doesn't exist. Regardless of whether it is understood, it is necessary to respect the other's experience. This goes for both partners.

5

Me? Us? No One? – Options and Choices for Sexual Pleasure

For some, there may be little or no sexual need whatsoever – either alone or with another person. When this is within a partner relationship, this can cause problems if it is not a mutual choice. For others, it may be that the social and emotional requirements of accommodating someone else's needs are either too complex to manage or not worth the compromise for the individual. Pornography can, for some, be part of a relationship, used as a substitute when not in a relationship, or be quite enough for some to achieve sexual satisfaction alone throughout their lives. These choices may be temporary or permanent and may change over time depending on personal circumstances. Like any population, there is no one set behaviour that 'works' for every person, for ever.

Pornography

Pornography is widely used by many people as a source of stimulation, either for solo masturbation or with a partner. The internet is the main source of this material with literally millions of pages online. The statistics website www.toptenreviews.com states that 12 per cent of all websites are pornography related, with over 28,000 internet users viewing porn every second. Men tend to use porn more frequently than women, which no doubt explains why there is so much more pornography aimed at men – both heterosexual and homosexual. Men tend to be more stimulated by visual images than women. In demographic studies cited on the above website, women are said to make up one-third of those accessing porn.

Whatever one's personal opinion on the use of pornography, it is big business, widely available and here to stay. In moderation, like most things, using porn to stimulate oneself can be harmless and useful as an alternative to being with a partner when one is not available. The danger for some people is that it can become an obsession and take up large amounts of time and money. Care also needs to be taken because some pornography is illegal and viewing it may lead to prosecution. Only images depicting consenting adults are acceptable (anything else is morally, socially and legally unacceptable in general society) and even then only in private. Some people find pornography degrading to women and distasteful to look at. Their views need to be respected.

For those with Asperger Syndrome (AS), who may have had little contact with sexual partners and limited social experiences, there may be the added issue that the behaviour and events in pornographic films may be taken as a realistic script for real life. Individuals may expect that they or others will behave in the same ways depicted – for example, that women are already prepared and available for sex with a series of strangers who arrive on their doorstep (this is often the script for porn films). In extreme cases, this can lead to a person being accused of sexual assault or deviancy (Attwood 2006). There may be a search for information and understanding about sex, which leads to porn in an attempt to obtain knowledge and facts (Attwood 2006).

Whether the viewing of pornography is viewed as being unfaithful or disrespectful to a partner is a personal decision. For many, it is simply a form of visual stimulation, which does not have an impact on feelings for a partner. Inappropriate use of porn – viewing illegal sites, using porn at work or where children may be able to see it – must be discussed and clear boundaries put into place. One man who responded had lost his job because of looking at porn at work where it had become an obsession and he had accrued a large collection of images on his work computer. The person with AS must understand that certain behaviour is unacceptable and will not be tolerated. This may be obvious to many people, but some people with AS will not naturally know that what they are doing is distressing or potentially harmful (Aston 2003).

Some of the men with AS who answered questions on this topic had huge collections of pornography, although this in no way suggests that they are different from the neuro-typical (NT) population. Some had very specific interests and preferences for material. Others had no interest in, nor had ever used pornographic material for stimulation; some viewed it as 'fake':

> I have a set of about two dozen pictures printed from free porn sites. Each is a picture of a single, slim woman in her 20s or early 30s, stripping or stripped, with reasonably sized breasts in full view, preferably pointing in the 1.00 or 11.00 direction with respect to the woman, where 12.00 is front and centre. When I masturbate, I usually group together a sub-set of these pictures with a similar quality – redheads, biggest breasts, outdoor poses…etc. (AS male)

> I have lots and lots of porn on my computer, thousands of pictures. It does not affect my sex life because I do not masturbate. When I forget myself and look at it when my wife is in the room, she is very unhappy about that. (AS male)

> I can enjoy the photos but do not really like videos. I get concerned about how the women involved in such things are treated when they are off camera. (AS female)

> I never looked at porn until I lived alone with access to the internet. Before then I had lived with others and couldn't trust them not to look at my things. (AS male)

> I use porn to help me masturbate. I use it the same amount as when I did whenever I was single. I suppose it might have an impact on my sexual relationships, but since my usage has not changed, I have no way to gauge its effect. (AS male)

> No demands were made upon me by the ladies in the magazines. (AS male)

> I have always used porn to a large extent, when I have wanted sexual relief, but haven't felt like I wanted it with my partner for whatever reason – bored with them/tired/

over-familiarity perhaps or even in a mood where I didn't want the physical contact. (AS male)

Even though I had a regular sex life with my wife, there was something about the illicitness of the material which made it exciting – forbidden fruit etc. (AS male)

No porn in my life. (AS male)

He (AS) tends to look at fetish porn...for the reason of 'seeing how it all works'. (NT female)

Porn has a strong place in my husband's (AS) life. I know he goes online to look at bondage photos all the time... I get pissed off, not because I am a prude about porn, but because at times it seems like an obsession with my husband. (NT female)

(He) (AS) has an unusual amount of pornographic material and enjoys it far more than I do but this doesn't bother me in the least. (NT female)

I do enjoy porn but my wife does not approve, so it's behind her back. If she were no longer my partner, I suspect I would use it more. (AS male)

I don't use it at all because in order for me to like something it needs to be real. Ninety per cent of porn is fake including the Photoshopped or surgery enhanced people. (AS female)

I use pornography of a soft-core nature to meet my sexual needs late at night when my wife is sleeping. I experience feelings of guilt, as I believe it is wrong, but it is the only sexual outlet I have at present. (AS male)

I did see intimate parts 'live', but it didn't make a great deal of impact in what was important in terms of what would make a good or feasible item to look at as possible relation-ship material. In fact, it is somewhat of a turn off as it leads to the question: how much of the assets are fake? We don't use porn currently. (AS male)

Porn was a way to ease my way into the idea of what might turn me on without the pressure or panic of a 'real-life' situation. (AS male)

My partner developed a severe problem with pornography…to the point he got himself fired when he got caught with it at work. The crisis this created in our marriage was equivalent to an actual affair in my view. (NT female)

Within a relationship, the use of pornography can prove upsetting for a partner who may see that their AS partner is more willing to engage in masturbation and watch sexually graphic images rather than initiate sex with them. Communication about personal needs and feelings round pornography is important. Each partner may have a very different perspective, which needs to be listened to and respected, even though this may be uncomfortable to do.

Masturbation

Masturbation is a normal activity for the majority of adults. The frequency and intensity of masturbating among those who responded to the questionnaire varied from never to several times each day. This range can be seen within the general population, although the all-or-nothing world view of a person with AS may make them more likely to abstain or indulge obsessively rather than take a more moderate, average line. Generally, this is not harmful unless it is engaged in publicly, inappropriately or to the exclusion of most other activities.

For some people, achieving satisfaction through masturbation is easier than trying to negotiate the complex communication required in initiating sex with their partner. Some possible reasons why a person may prefer masturbation to sex with a partner may be:

- the possibility of rejection if asking for sex with a partner
- a need to retain control of sexual arousal

- the fear of 'getting it wrong' and causing the partner to become upset or angry
- non-verbal signals that may be misread about what type of sexual activity is desired
- a need for simple physical release and not being able to engage socially and emotionally with another person
- a requirement to meet the sexual needs of the partner when the person only wants to focus on their own needs
- sensory stimulation that may make close physical contact uncomfortable
- the emotional intimacy of another person, which may be overwhelming
- anxiety about performance.

Those who responded to the questionnaire were very open about their experiences of and motivations for masturbating:

> Masturbation with porn is unfortunately the best sex I've ever had. It is easy. The two-dimensional women are there and ready. I don't need to worry about the social difficulties involved with the steps before, during and after sex with a three-dimensional woman. (AS male, virgin)

> For many years my husband (AS) preferred to masturbate 5+ times a week while rejecting my advances. After many tears and some counselling he stopped masturbating but seems to have chosen celibacy instead. (NT female)

> I suppose the need for masturbation is because I feel quite sexual a lot of the time, but don't want to get too involved with someone for all the other things a relationship entails (sharing, compromise, lack of personal freedom). If I can get my sexual satisfaction out of the way by myself, I can then do what I like for the rest of the day without taking anyone else's feelings into account. (AS male)

I've always felt sex to be overrated. During some brief periods in life, I've indulged in masturbation more than once a day. However, in general, once daily to once every few days tends to be sufficient. (AS male)

One thing I prefer during masturbation at night is the warm glow of a carbon-filament lamp dimmed with a variable transformer… The light bulb, when dimmed properly, emits the same intensity and reddish hue as a romantic candle flame. (AS male)

First sexual experiences were self-bondage and masturbation at age ten. (AS male)

He (AS) needs me to give him pleasure; he will not masturbate and take on the responsibility for his own pleasure no matter how tired, overwhelmed or sick I am. (NT female)

He (AS) can only orgasm with masturbation. (NT female)

He (AS) will masturbate to go to sleep. If he does not do this, he is really tired or depressed. (NT female)

I have an extremely high sex drive which I satisfy with masturbation when no partner is around. Also means I don't have to be social with someone if I don't fancy it. I have frequent fantasies about people I have met or who I work with. Gets me through the day. (AS male)

He (AS) has had periods where he prefers masturbation to actual intercourse with me, and oral sex rather than intercourse. (NT female)

I masturbate about three times a week. I haven't had sex with my wife in three years (since our wedding night). (AS male)

I was a late bloomer and didn't start masturbating until 18 or 19. (AS male)

Fantasy and imagination

One of the criteria for AS is the less developed ability to imagine abstract and unreal concepts and ideas, and yet many individuals report having excellent visualisation skills and a well-developed fantasy life. This range is probably typical of the general population, some of whom do fantasise either alone when masturbating or during sex with their partners. This is quite normal behaviour – whether you do or whether you don't – and can be shared with a partner or kept private. Some partners may prefer not to know if you are thinking about someone else while having sex with them. If the fantasy involves them, they may like to hear about it:

> I have no sexual fantasies at all. (AS male)

> I have been upset with my husband (AS) fantasising about other women and making a list of the women he wanted to sleep with, including friends of mine… It took me a long time to understand that it was beneath his developmental level to understand the boundaries without help. I had to send him to a therapist, and that is how we managed to work things out. I went to a counsellor myself and that was also helpful. (NT female)

> I stooped so low as to create an imaginary girlfriend. I named her _____. I drew a small picture of her wearing sloppy clothes, with messy hair, a big smile and focused eyes. (AS male)

> I do not fantasise at all and I know that he (AS) doesn't either. I like the fact that we are both completely 'present' and focused on what is happening between us when we make love and not thinking about someone or something else. (NT female)

Virtual sex/phone sex

The culture of meeting people over the internet can include sexual conversation either online via websites or messenger services or by telephone. The impersonal and anonymous nature of the internet can make it easier for some people to obtain sexual stimulation with someone they have never met. It is mutually pleasurable, free and a lot less complicated than having a relationship. As long as mutual consent and legal issues (contact with minors) are addressed, some people find this a welcome alternative to solo masturbation. It can also form part of a relationship when partners are not together. One AS woman met partners after having phone or online sex with them and then began more conventional relationships in person.

A man with AS liked to talk about sex all the time and had been told that he offended people on online chat services. He enjoyed phone sex with his wife but said that she didn't like to do it as the kids were usually around. This person was unable to prioritise between his immediate desires and the well-being of his children who were exposed to his sexual behaviour. This could be seen as a characteristic of the self-focused perspective of some with AS, which may result from less developed empathy skills, rather than a deliberate intent to harm his children. Most of those with AS expressed no desire for this type of stimulation and some simply did not get the attraction. This type of conversation may rely on an element of fantasy, which some with AS say that they do not, or cannot, engage in:

> It can be fun but sometimes it is nice to actually be with a person and feel their touch. In the absence of the opportunity for physical sex, virtual, especially with voice is nice. Voice is a big turn on for me. (AS female)

> (He) (AS) is very averse to any 'sex talk' between us on the phone or online… It makes him uncomfortable and he doesn't know how to respond to it. (NT female)

Celibacy/remaining alone

Having a negative experience in a relationship seems to have the effect of causing some with AS to withdraw completely from all possible encounters, sometimes for several years. Some people simply do not have the confidence to initiate a first relationship. The individual may already have low self-esteem from a lifetime of misunderstanding and lack of success in social endeavours, which is further damaged by another perceived 'failure' or the fear of being hurt or overwhelmed. Perhaps having fewer peers with whom to discuss and deal with the feelings and put an encounter into perspective means that the individual has to manage all their emotions alone.

Living in an all-or-nothing binary state as many with AS do, relationships can be seen as great or terrible and not viewed realistically. The end of a relationship, no matter how brief, means that things have changed, are unpredictable and are now 'different'. This in itself can be a stressful concept to assimilate. Reading books or websites on getting over relationships and discussing what happened with others on forums or in person can help to make sense of things. There are two people in any relationship and therefore the blame for its end is rarely entirely the fault of only one person. If someone decides that they no longer wish to be in a relationship with you, it does not mean that you are deficient. Most people have more than one relationship in their lives and thus most relationships must end in order for new ones to begin. Learning from each experience and moving on positively is the best way to make the most of every sad situation. This doesn't mean that feelings should be shut off and ignored because they may surface again at a later date or become repressed. Feeling sad, angry or afraid is quite typical and these feelings do pass in time. Allow yourself some time to process your feelings rather than swiftly moving on to find another partner or shutting yourself away fearing another 'failure'. A relationship ending is not a 'failure': people change, circumstances change and the relationship may no longer be able to keep up with those changes:

> He (AS) chose it (celibacy) after the breakdown of his first relationship and went into (seven) years of mourning. (NT female)

> Fear of failure or rejection affects ability and desire… I remained alone for seven years. (AS male)

> My husband (AS) says he was involved with a crazy older woman who pursued him… When it ended my husband pierced his own penis, as some kind of act of what he said would be a commitment to life-long abstinence. (NT female)

> There was a period of time after the marriage split, where my self-confidence was so shaken. I had trouble approaching women for three to four years. (AS male)

All those who had been married and divorced and were now single expressed no desire to be part of a long-term, live-in relationship again. Some chose to have sexual encounters, but were wary of sharing space with someone:

> I do like regular sex, but am not prepared to sacrifice too much of my own wishes to get it. (AS male)

> I'm very aware of the tangles in male/female AS/NT couples which would make me very careful about sleeping with anyone. In general, I'm pretty vulnerable at this time and couldn't tolerate much more risk and complexity. (AS male)

> I've learned that I don't want to be in a relationship. Had I known I had AS three years ago, I would never have married. (AS male)

> I'm too self-sufficient… Certainly I have lost all trust that I could ever make a woman happy. Ultimately my relationships with women have been intellectual encounters, with a façade of sexual play acting. (AS male)

> Two years now with no sex, and no prospects. (AS male)

There is a sense of life being less complicated alone than with a partner – to the extent that some people in relationships who answered the questionnaire wished they had remained alone. The urge and desire to be part of a relationship seems to be a greater driving force for NT partners who perhaps don't experience the same stress and confusion. Not being able to do as one chooses was seen as a definite loss by some AS partners and this overshadowed any benefits of being in a relationship:

> Low self-esteem was one reason I hung on so hard to a relationship that was bad for me. I am not currently looking for a serious relationship. (AS female)

Of course it is easier to be alone because relationships are more complicated than your own life by itself. (AS male)

(I have) a reluctance to do things with a partner in which I may not have the slightest interest; also, not being able to please myself whenever I want to do something by myself. (AS male)

Now I don't drink, I'm still coming around to the idea that I'm not meant to be with any one person – just pick and choose the parts of relationships that fill my needs without being totally responsible for someone else's happiness. (AS male)

Yes, (it is) easier to remain out of relationships. I generally like things to stay the same and don't mind repetitive behaviours/situations. (AS male)

I sometimes wonder: what's the point? (AS male)

I'm just not interested. It's a bloody pain to have to look out for other people all the time. (AS male)

The end of a relationship is not just about the severing of emotional ties from the partner; it's about losing the life that being with that person enabled me to lead: the social network that we built up together, the motivation and initiation of social engagements, the organisation of finances and general daily life and all of the other skills she had that I simply don't. Although I am probably able to do some of these things on my own, I don't; I simply lack the motivation. (AS male)

Virginity

Only two people who responded had not had a sexual relationship so far and they were both men with AS in their mid to late 20s. A greater number of individuals with AS had not had their first sexual experience until much later than their NT peers. The views of those who were still virgins differed from being unconcerned and unmotivated to find a partner to being depressed and obsessed in doing so. The following comments are thoughts from the two individuals who responded:

No loss of virginity yet and no anxiety about that. (AS male)

I do not choose to remain single, but merely lack the motivation required to expend the effort required to bring about a change in the situation. (AS male)

The motivation to find sexual partners has never been sufficient to overcome the social anxiety. (AS male)

Some men can brag that they had a threesome. I'd just be happy with a twosome. (AS male)

On my first time I would be curious to compare the parts of the breasts and vulva with what I have had to teach myself on Wikipedia. (AS male)

There are many people with AS who have not had any sexual experiences with another person throughout their adult life. Temple Grandin, an acclaimed writer, professor of animal science and speaker on autism, took the decision not to have relationships as a positive choice. She felt that, as she looked around her at people in relationships, she couldn't see one that she could fit herself into. She said that she needed a template; she couldn't imagine what it would be like (personal communication). She also believes that the only AS relationships that work are those where there are strong shared interests or where the other partner also has traits of AS. Temple Grandin has chosen to remain celibate in order to avoid complicated social situations that she cannot manage. Physical closeness to another person is also an issue for her (Grandin 1996). She has chosen instead to focus on her work and projects, which give her a sense of fulfilment. Temple demonstrates her awareness that she is undoubtedly missing something but she has replaced emotional complexity with intellectual complexity, which for her works well.

Whether one is anxious about lack of sexual activity or not, it is important to establish a fulfilling life for oneself regardless. Many people in long-term relationships have fairly infrequent sex and do not consider it to be very important. However, to others it may seem hugely significant purely because it is an unobtainable pleasure. Finding enjoyment in other activities can help avoid the pursuit of sex becoming an overwhelming fascination or a source of depression.

Prostitutes

Three men with AS (8%) had had experiences with prostitutes and one said that he would prefer sex with someone he didn't have to respect (as opposed to his wife) because that was easier for him. His first experiences had been with a prostitute. This type of business transaction may suit some people because it does not require the social skills necessary to negotiate friendship prior to sex. A sex worker may also be less judgemental and more understanding with a nervous or socially awkward person:

> I've never been interested in relationships, although the fact that I didn't have a girlfriend became a problem as people thought it was weird. The prostitutes were an attempt to get used to girls. (AS male)

> Many (encounters) have been with prostitutes. (AS male)

> I'd like to have sexual relations with a woman I don't respect. Or perhaps it's better to say with someone who had no expectations beyond the sex act. (AS male)

Care needs to be taken as to the legality of such an arrangement as well as any health or safety considerations. Seeking the services of a sex worker is illegal in some countries and may result in arrest. If you do choose to do so, finding licensed premises is recommended. In some areas, prostitutes work by waiting on streets to be picked up by people in their cars. Unless you are absolutely sure that you know that someone is a prostitute, it is unadvisable to approach anyone on the street with requests for sex because this is very likely to lead to arrest. There will be sexual health services within your locality that may be able to advise more specifically on how to go about finding a sex worker.

AS and NT women

Promiscuous sexual behaviour is sometimes seen in women with AS (Attwood 2006; Hénault 2006) and it has been identified earlier that the AS females who completed the questionnaire had sex at a younger age than their male or NT female counterparts. This may be caused by having poor personal boundaries and understanding of the motivations of partners. This seems to be more common for AS women than males and may be due to differences between genders in the need for acceptance and approval from others. For a socially isolated young woman, the attention of males is a new and exciting occurrence and an opportunity to appear 'normal' and socially accepted.

Tony Attwood comments that women with AS may be more vulnerable because they are less able to read the complex unspoken signals involved in sexual relationships, and have fewer friends with whom to discuss and learn to identify sexual predators (Attwood 2006). A woman with AS may believe what she is told by a potential partner, when he may simply be saying anything in order to have sex with her. More socially aware women would be able to 'read between the lines' and avoid dangerous and predatory partners. Half the women with AS reported that they had experienced some form of abusive sexual situation; therefore, it is important that women with AS find support from others who can advise on what is safe behaviour. If you have experienced this type of situation, know that it was not your fault and that there are trained counsellors who can allow you to talk about your experiences in confidence. This can be very helpful.

Unless you are looking for a purely sexual relationship, it is useful advice to wait for some time before having sex with a new partner. If they really want a relationship with you, they will be happy to wait. If they only want to have sex and nothing more, they will not stay around. This is better than having sex with someone who then does not return your calls, which is confusing and upsetting. It is also important to take responsibility for your own sexual health, contraception and personal boundaries (what is OK and not OK for you). Sexual health clinics have leaflets and advisors who can provide detailed information. Two respondents described upsetting early experiences:

> My first experiences were not willing. I lost my virginity at age 14 to my cousin…rape. I misread cues and ended up in situations where dates expected sex and I froze and could not fight them. I got pregnant at age 16 as a result of one of those encounters. (AS female)

> I became the sex object for boys and men who took advantage of my inability to understand what were 'grown-up' games and what was inappropriate for children. (AS female)

As well as the women with AS just quoted, five NT female respondents mentioned a history of some form of sexual attack or pressure. This was not directly asked in the questionnaire. This represents almost one-third of those women who responded. In view of the potential distress that following up these disclosures may cause, and the inability of the author to ensure the well-being of participants due to the remote nature of this research, no questions regarding abuse were asked of these or other participants in order to assess whether this was a more widespread occurrence.

Perhaps the gentleness and non-macho traits that are often described in AS men are specifically attractive to women who have experienced sexual assault from a more predatory male figure in their lives. It is not possible to draw any conclusions from such limited information, but this may be an interesting area for further study.

6

Statistics of Sex

So, at what age is it 'normal' to first have sex? And how many partners should a person have? As with any group, the answer is not conclusive and nor does it seek to be: the ages at which those with Asperger Syndrome (AS) lose their virginity, and the frequency and head count of partners, all vary and depend on the circumstances of each individual. Some people report regular and satisfying sexual relationships with one or several partners, while others find their intimacy by way of shared interests and companionships and have no physical relationships at all. Whether this is satisfactory to each individual varies from one person to another: what is right for someone else may not be right for you. Try to resist the temptation to compare yourself with others for they are not you:

> He (AS) is by far the best lover I have ever had. Despite the fact that he was a very late-starter – in his 30s – and has had only a small number of partners, he is wonderful: attentive, always willing, emotionally close and very adept. This part of our relationship makes up for the difficulties elsewhere. (NT female)

> My partner allows me to grope her whenever. It shows that she is at ease with me and I know I will not be rejected. It is a nice feeling; playful and fun. (AS male)

With a supportive partner and good communication, it can be possible to have a satisfactory sexual and emotional life for both partners, whatever your level of experience. One partner said that he had worked out that sex was a matter of both parties getting what they wanted and that he had a better chance of getting what he wanted by ensuring that his partner's needs were met – both sexually and emotionally. Appreciating this reciprocity, which many people with AS find difficult, benefits both parties. If one person expects to behave exactly as they choose with no consideration for their partner's needs, the relationship will suffer. Even if the person with AS does not understand the needs of their partner, it is essential that they listen and respond wherever possible. A neuro-typical (NT) partner needs to be more explicit about their emotional requirements because the AS partner may be unable to guess what is needed or desired.

First experiences

Given the difficulties in socialising and locating and engaging a partner, it is not surprising that some men with AS do not have their first sexual experience until considerably later than average, and some have no sexual experiences with another person throughout their lives. This seems to be less applicable to the women with AS in our study, who all had their first experiences in their teens. Perhaps this is due to the expectation that men will initiate sexual relations, and that this makes it easier for women with AS to find partners. Interestingly, some of the NT partners had also decided to wait until later in life to have sex for the first time, and had chosen an AS partner to share this with. Seventeen per cent of the NT women were over 30 when they had their first experience, and they were all still with that partner who had AS, whether male or female. This seems quite unusual and suggests that the person with AS may be seen as safe in some way by these women who have chosen to wait:

> Intercourse, 41, with my now husband. It counts more.
> Worth the wait and all the tea in China. (NT female)

Otherwise, over 60 per cent of the NT women had had their first sexual experiences by the age of 20, whereas for the men with AS only 50 per cent had done so by the same age.

The ages of first sexual experience ranged from 12 to 37 in the AS males who answered the question and 14 to 19 for the AS females (although this was a much smaller sample). Across the NT females the range was 13 to 41. No NT males completed the questionnaire. The majority of scores were between 17 and 33 for AS males and 18 to 22 for

NT females. Around 50 per cent of AS males had had their first experience between the ages of 18 to 26. Almost 40 per cent were aged 26 or over at the time of their first sexual encounter. The NT females showed that 50 per cent were between 18 to 20 years at the time of their first sexual experience, and fewer than 20 per cent had sex for the first time at 26 years or older. The four AS women who answered this question had all had their first experience prior to the age of 19, 50 per cent of them at 14 years of age – considerably younger than average or legally permissible.

These results show that there are some differences between the groups. Those most likely to have sex at a younger age were AS females, followed by NT females with AS males having their first sex at a later age.

It was expected that there would be significant differences in age of first consensual sexual experience between AS and NT respondents, although these were not as significant as predicted. This may be that this is a skewed sample of people, most of whom are currently in relationships and so have managed to negotiate a sexual encounter. From the author's professional experience, a large majority of clients worked with are known not to have had any sexual relationships throughout their lifetime and, had this group contributed data, the results would look very different.

Although it can be distressing for a person to feel that they desire a relationship or sexual experience but will never have one, it is important to keep this in perspective. Many people find it difficult to maintain relationships in current society and there are many single people who would prefer not to be so – regardless of whether they have AS. Spending one's time and energy keeping challenged, active and interested in making contact with other people is the best way to attract interesting people. Self-awareness, enjoyment of life and confidence are attractive features. These non-verbal signals are readable by a NT person who will be able to 'sense' if someone is happy with their lives and confident in themselves, or is desperate for a partner – which is generally not seen as attractive. Speaking to someone trustworthy is useful in learning about how the NT world works.

There can be a sense of pressure and expectation from family and friends who may show interest or concern as to why a girl/boyfriend is not forthcoming:

> The personal questions from adults within my family embarrassed me by asking if I had a girlfriend. It felt like an attack rather than interest. What's it got to do with you? How dare you ask me, was how I felt. (AS male)

Some people do not have their first sexual experiences until their 30s or 40s, despite the media that suggest that everyone is getting lots of sex. Added to this is the stigma of admitting that you are not, and hence there are a lot of people lying about the true extent of their sexual encounters. It is important for individuals not to believe everything that they hear and follow the path that is right for them, even if this is different from that of their peers. Some people with AS can be particularly vulnerable and easily led into behaviour that may cause further difficulties and anxiety. Having a strong sense of self is vital for maintaining self-esteem and confidence. Having a sexual relationship is only one aspect of a balanced life and should only be accorded a proportion of one's thought and energies. It should also be remembered that for some people being in a relationship means sacrificing some of one's interests, and time, for those of someone else, which may be especially difficult for someone with AS due to a potentially greater sense of self-interest and requirement for certain routines and stability.

One of the factors that may inhibit early sexual relationships is an emotional immaturity said to be exhibited in those with AS in comparison to NT peers of the same age (Aston 2003; Attwood 2006). This is freely admitted in some individuals and not intended to be offensive. This can be accompanied by less knowledge of sexual matters (Hénault 2006) than would be expected due to a smaller peer network of potential partners. There may be an intellectual knowledge of biological bodily functions, but not as an emotional or social concept:

> I am boyish both mentally and physically. (AS male)

> I am an emotional teenager. I guess that, like most teenagers, when I have what I think is a great idea I leap up and want to put it into action immediately. When others say 'Not now, let's do it another time' I feel great rage and frustration. I want to do it now – why on earth don't they? What's the point in waiting? (AS male)

So, although the person is physically adult, their capacity to relate emotionally is of a younger person (Moxon (2001) in Lawson 2005)). This may mean that sexual interest may be present but it is more reminiscent of an adolescent in nature, despite more advanced years, and therefore results in a reduced ability to attract a willing partner due to the appearance of being childish and immature. Some NT female partners commented on this aspect of their partner. Examples of the behaviour described included a constant groping of breasts, a child-like fascination with the partner's body and a refusal to discuss personal subjects. Some female partners felt that their partner was like an extra child in the family and a drain on their energy. Others felt that these qualities were playful and endearing and saw them as positive traits. There is some evidence that suggests that life becomes easier for those with AS once they reach their late 20s (Attwood 2002). In some ways, this is true of many people: some suggest that a sense of self-acceptance often accompanies the approach of 30. There are also issues with the requirements of socialising at a younger age. Perhaps potential partners become more tolerant as age increases and things such as having problems at parties and in large groups become less important and the qualities of those with AS – knowledge, stability and reliability – become more valued. As for anyone, a whole host of factors determines the circumstances of sexual encounters, or the decision not to indulge:

> He (AS) said that he was willing to have sex with me (at age 37 years) after many years of saying no to many girls because he liked me and felt comfortable. He had an attraction towards me that he had not felt before. (NT female)

> Someone I have been at university with ten years previously made her interest known. The sheer fact that she was interested in me was enough – an opportunity to investigate further. Don't know if I was attracted to her. I was more interested in the mechanics. It was probably not satisfactory for either party. I have no strong memories of the occasion. (AS male, first sexual experience at age 31 years)

> First experience initiated by partner at age 16. Hadn't really considered it previously, just went along with it. (AS male)

No loss of virginity yet and no anxiety about that. (AS male, 29)

My partner (AS) was 18 and 'seduced' by the mother of a schoolmate (she was about 25 years his senior). (NT female)

On my wedding day with my wife at age 23. My first masturbation to orgasm was at age 22. (AS male)

I chanced to find myself sharing a bed with a voluptuous redhead, got a massive hard-on, she was interested, got nervous half-way through and lost the erection. (AS male)

Honeymoon at age 32. I had had a couple of other relationships before I started courting the lady who I was to marry; because I was a committed Christian we did not have sexual relations. (AS male)

Late 20s with a prostitute. (AS male)

For some, there was a resignation that sex was never going to happen to them. This may be simply an acceptance of the fact or alternatively may cause depression or result in obsessive interests and behaviour:

I tried to be sexless throughout my 20s, to ban all desires and emotions. I stopped any thoughts of this nature by a matter of will. There was a yearning when masturbating to be close to someone. I was resigned to the fact that it was never going to happen. This wasn't a troubling daily issue, just an un-emotive fact. (AS male, first sexual experience at 31 years old)

By the time I met my husband I was pretty well convinced I would never understand anyone well enough to maintain something everlasting. (AS female)

For a very long time I believed I was a hopeless case. 'How could anyone love me?' I just wanted one person to walk beside me and accept me for who I was. (AS female)

I knew celibacy would not happen. Would it take time? Yes. I just got very fortunate that I didn't have to wait until I was 50 years old to find someone that would make me so excited as to not consider being alone any more; that was the hard part. (AS male)

For others, the desire to have a relationship may result in its becoming an all-encompassing obsession and the only topic of conversation. It may be hard to imagine that the object of their desire doesn't feel the same way that they do and they may behave inappropriately to that person. This behaviour is discussed later in this book. One man with AS in his 40s remembered a woman he had known at college and still believed that if he could find her they would be together despite the fact that there had been no contact for 20 years. He had not been able to establish a relationship throughout his life despite expressing a desire for one. It is unclear as to whether he was fully aware of the requirements of being a partner, as opposed to having one. Some people have unusual and unrealistic expectations of relationships, which may not be shared.

Emotional attachment

Participants were asked whether they considered it necessary to be emotionally attached (have loving feelings) to someone in order to have sex with them or is sex a purely physical act and entirely separate from love. Overwhelmingly, the majority of men with AS who answered the question (71%) said that no, it wasn't necessary and that sex and emotions were quite separate.

Almost the exact opposite statistics were seen in the NT female sample with 94 per cent saying that emotional attachment was either necessary or preferable. Only one NT woman said that they were separate.

Out of the four AS women who answered the question, two said sex with emotional attachment was preferable and two said that attachment was not required for sex. None of the AS women said that the two were necessary. This is seen in other research (Aston 2003). This is a more straightforward viewpoint than for most NT women who attached an emotional importance to the physical act. If the person with AS doesn't read body language or value the illogical emotional aspects of the relationship, sex may be more utilitarian and less romantic (Stanford 2003). For some NTs (especially women), there is an emotional element required before engaging in sex. This difference in agenda can cause difficulties if both parties assume that the other person shares their value system and believes sex to be meaningful/meaningless depending on their position:

> The most important thing is the absence of negative emotions and stress. No sense of sexual chemistry ever. No sense of 'lovemaking'. (AS male)

> Sex is physical and does not require emotional feelings for a person. (AS male)

> Sexually, I (NT) often had the feeling that I could have been anyone – I felt no emotional connection from him (AS). (NT female)

> What the body needs and what the spirit needs is different at different times. (AS female)

> Sex is different from love. (AS male)

> I can't shake the feeling that there should be more to it. I cannot seem to grasp it though, even though I try. (AS male)

> Emotional attachment and sex are two separate issues. The physical act is more of a sensory and biological need. (AS female)

Not all the AS respondents agreed that sex was just as satisfactory without emotional attachment to the partner. Some people had only had one partner throughout their lives and others – both those who had had no sexual partners and those who had had more than one – felt that emotional feelings were required for sex. Others said that, although they felt that the physical and emotional sides of sex were separate, sex was preferable if feelings for the person were present:

> If it is not there (emotional attachment) it is just a hollow exercise in installing electronic wiring. (AS male)

I need some emotional attachment to make it worth it. Otherwise it seems like mutual masturbation. (AS male)

I'm not capable of telling if the other person has an emotional attachment to me or not, but as long as I do then sex can proceed. (AS female)

Emotionally close is easier than physically close. (AS male)

Even if it's originally just a physical act emotions end up being attached after sex. (AS female)

There is no physical difference in the experience but sex is preferable with someone that you love. (AS male)

Yes, in almost all practical cases in my life, it's a meeting of souls. (AS male)

Generally, some kind of profound bonding is at stake (even for a week!). In AS-land, a week is a long time. (AS male)

If I found that I had a one-night stand with someone who I later disliked, I would feel stupid and also angry with myself for following my appetites, instead of getting to know the person on an intellectual level first, which has usually been my way in the past. (AS male)

How many partners?

Statistics into sexual behaviour within the population as a whole are understandably unreliable. People may be cautious about revealing details of their sexual behaviour, especially if it is not perceived to be typical. It is common belief that men are more prone to exaggerate the number of sexual partners, where women will decrease the number. This is a reflection on conflicting societal attitudes to sex depending on gender. A man with many partners may be seen to be admired, whereas a woman may not be looked on so favourably.

Numbers of sexual partners of those questioned varied. Again, it must be noted that these are mostly people who have had relationships and do not include large numbers of the AS population who have not had any partners. Some respondents did not give an exact figure for the number of partners using a subjective phrase like: 'Too many to count'. Those who had had up to ten partners were able to give this as a definitive total and so 'too many to count' was presumed to be above this figure. No person who had more than ten partners gave a figure, but instead indicated that the precise number was unknown.

When looking at the numbers of partners for AS males, almost 50 per cent had 0 to 2 partners. Another 40 per cent had 5 or more partners. Less than 15 per cent had 10+ partners and all these mentioned a problem with alcohol, although this issue was specifically raised.

The AS females who responded had between 4 and 10+ partners. Thirty per cent of NT females had 0 to 2 partners. Over 60 per cent of NT females had 5 or more partners with 25 per cent having 10 or more.

In general the men with AS had fewer partners than the NT and AS females. The AS female sample was very small (four respondents) and the numbers of partners are more typical of NT females than of AS males (75% having 5 or more partners).

7

Asperger Syndrome Between the Sheets

What do couples with Asperger Syndrome (AS) get up to in the bedroom? Those who responded to the questionnaires were surprisingly open and willing to reveal their pleasures and annoyances in the bedroom. There were areas of commonality for several people and these have been looked at in some detail.

Routines

One of the main characteristics of AS is a need for structure, routine and sameness and so for some sexual interaction is no exception. Flexibility, spontaneity and variation are not on the agenda for these individuals, much to their partners' dismay, on some occasions. Others with AS and their partners reported an enjoyment of variety in their sexual lives. Perhaps the safe environment of being with a long-term, trusted partner allows for less stress than everyday life for some people:

> If anything he (AS) focuses too hard, once finding a certain thing that works he does it over and over until given another thing that works. (AS female)

> With a set routine, I would be most comfortable and able to perform. But routine drives wife crazy. (AS male)

> For a long time, sex had to be scheduled. I could not approach him (AS) about it on a day that he had to work. I

could not interrupt him while he was working on his computer or watching a hockey game. (NT female)

I like to play around and try new things. (AS female)

I find the same routine boring and mechanical. I am willing to experience new things, but nothing odd or kinky. (AS male)

He does seem to fall back into a routine. He's content to follow each step every time. When asked to do something new he seems uncomfortable. (NT female)

Some things are better than others. I'm willing to try things beyond my scope of preference, but ultimately there are a core set of activities that I return to, because I find I like them. (AS male)

I often feel that I want to change things but I find it hard – no imagination. (AS male)

We have only had routine sex. I find much of my stimulation to be mental. (AS male)

My wife and I never had anything like a fixed routine for sex. Patterns changed year to year: at bedtime, in the morning, in the afternoon, in the living room. Oral sex, randy fucking. A French forest with pine needles and ants! An Australian beach at night. (AS male)

For him (AS) to be able to come (orgasm) he has to follow a set routine. For some time it was also the same for him to get an erection. Once we worked on this he got incredibly good at it but he did extensive reading to master it. (NT female)

I don't like a set routine during sex. I like things to be different. (AS male)

He (AS) prefers a set routine, a planned night, and the exact same quick sex in the same position. (NT female)

Partner as experiment/plaything

Several people commented on their partner's almost clinical, exploratory fascination with their bodies; some enjoyed this attention and others found it invasive and disrespectful. It seems that some of this interest fits with the AS personality of being interested in how things work and what happens when one performs a certain action (stimulation). It is possible that for some with AS there has been limited contact with a naked body and thus it is a relatively new or limited experience. The emotional immaturity that some with AS are said to display (and some admit to) may also result in a somewhat teenage attitude to the partner's body. Finding a balance for each partner where touch can be enjoyed and appreciated as a sign of attraction and affection, but where it is not unpleasant for either party, is important:

> Partner (AS) spent hours playing with my body, which should have been wonderful, but it was for his own enjoyment. Even when I asked him to stop he would carry on and tell me that I liked it really. I felt like an experiment; an investigation. (NT female)

> I would have to remind him (AS) that it was my body not his personal plaything. (NT female)

> I love to play with my wife's breasts – I would love to have breasts of my own! Her reactions do not fascinate me as much as her various parts do. (AS male)

> At times I think my husband (AS) isn't making love; he is using me as his 'plaything'. (NT female)

> At first it was something to be investigated. Now I have explored it and it's not interesting any more. (AS male)

> Different people react to the same types of touch and stimulation in different ways. This is very interesting to play with and observe and experiment with. (AS female)

> The partners' reactions always did fascinate me. So I played up to this to give her the greatest pleasure. Though the

spiritual and emotional aspects were undoubtedly absent, I endeavoured at least to pretend to the passion I'd never experienced. (AS male)

My partner is to be investigated. It has certain parts that are absolutely unique to this person... Their reactions to my investigating lead to some interesting ideas. I am made more curious by her erogenous zones. (AS male)

I regard partners' bodies as something to be shared with each other for mutual enjoyment. I wish my wife would respond more openly when I stimulate her. (AS male)

I find it fascinating to watch her breasts wobble. It could be any part of the body but her breasts are the most pendulous. I enjoy the response when I prod them. When you press something rapidly the impulse of energy is likely to give a resonant wobble. I am interested to see if it will do this so I do it again. I could become obsessed with pressing, getting a reaction and doing it again! I do it because I know she will let me. (AS male)

We have been divorced for five years. He (AS) still touches my breasts when he visits the house to collect the children. I have given up shouting at him as this has no effect. Last time I calmly asked him not to do it. He said: 'Why?' I said: 'Because they are mine'. He thought for a second, nodded and seemed to concede to that as a valid reason. He hasn't done it since. (NT female)

Meeting partners' needs

If a person with AS obtains stimulation from certain sexual practices, they may find it difficult, or impossible, to believe that their partner may find the same activity unpleasant, uncomfortable or painful, but this may well be the case. All individuals find pleasure and enjoyment from different sensations. This may stem from a difficulty appreciating that others have different thoughts, feelings and preferences from the person with AS – a less developed sense of empathy, which is said to accompany AS:

It seems to offend him (AS) if I gently move his hand to where it is good for me. We don't discuss it much. (NT female)

I'd like a more natural meshing feeling where I don't have to steer intimate encounters in an emotionally connecting direction so much, but I think this will continue to get better with time. (NT female)

I think both of us are frustrated with our sex life. We each want more of our own needs met and consequently don't end up having as much sex as we would like. (NT female)

I occasionally sense that (he) (AS) feels a pressure to 'perform' for me, but we also have plenty of encounters that aren't 'goal oriented' in which he's free to do whatever he likes and orgasm whenever and however he wants. (NT female)

(He) (AS) was very focused at the beginning of our sexual life as a couple to achieve orgasms as evidence that we were having good sex. Later in life...he has slowly come to understand other kinds of intimacy. (NT female)

(My) AS partner didn't like me to initiate sex – he'd withdraw or push me away. (NT female)

I would ask him (AS) to stop what he was doing because I found it uncomfortable or painful. He would say sorry, stop for a moment or two and then start again doing the same thing. He seemed unable to understand that it wasn't as enjoyable for me as it was for him. It was as though he thought I was lying. (NT female)

Some people only find specific sensations arousing and fail to comprehend why their partner may need a different touch or area of the body stimulated. Their willingness to reciprocate pleasure may be absent because they can't see what's in it for them, although many people have stated that their AS partner goes to great lengths to ensure they are satisfied sexually as long as this is clearly communicated – they are unable to guess or read the non-verbal signs that a sexual partner is enjoying themselves. Even understanding that a partner may just want to be close rather than sexual may need to be clearly stated as the AS partner may find it difficult to differentiate between the signals for sexual affection and emotional affection. These are subtle signals, which are often difficult for anyone to read, so it is important that neither partner blames the other for not being able to do so:

> The concept is easy; it's a matter of understanding that sex is a shared process, everyone wants to get the most out of it, and I find that that can be assured if I provide what is required. This applies to the satisfaction of emotional as well as physical needs. The actual mechanics are also easy, it's all a matter of action and response; response is generally immediate and not hard to interpret. It's a situation that provides me with enough information to function well in. If only people were just as responsive in social situations then the world would be a lot simpler place for me to exist in! (AS male)

> I find it much more of a turn on to make my partner feel good in bed than to have it happen to me. I feel unworthy of such stuff inside and squirm a bit inside my head. I can't wait to 'turn the tables' and make my partner feel really aroused, which in turn arouses me. (AS male)

> He just did not want to walk away without me climaxing (he had read that if a woman is not satisfied a relationship deteriorates, boy was I lucky he took it as a rule!). (NT female)

> He was 50 per cent me, me, me, me and 50 per cent I want to please because it makes me feel good if I make you crazy. (He) took my orgasms as a personal achievement... Being a good lover made him feel good and successful. (NT female)

> I consider my sexual relationship with (him) to be a good one, because he was willing to read if he did not know something. (NT female)

How much? How often?

Research has shown that 45–50 per cent (Aston 2003; Jacobs 2006) of couples, where one or more partners have AS, have no sexual relationship. Other couples have a very regular and varied sex life. It does seem that there is a mismatch between many couples, where one partner wants considerably more or less sex than the other, and this appears to cause a lot of distress and difficulty for these couples:

> I like to do something about it three to four times a week. I think I want sex often because I crave the closeness and hope that sex will bring it, but it doesn't. (NT female)

> We do not live together, so do not share the everyday stresses of life. We have sex every time we see each other, sometimes more than once a day. We have been together for over three years and this has never diminished. (NT female)

> I have a healthy sex drive. It does not need to be 'talked to' (stroked) very often in order to get certain things out of it. (AS male)

> I have a high sex drive. I want sex every day no matter what. I wish my wife would want more sex like I do. (AS male)

> High sex drive. If I don't have sexual stimuli I will dream it. (AS female)

> I consider myself to have a high and consistent sexual 'interest' and 'curiosity'. I do value regular sexual stimulation at least from erotic images and photos. (AS male)

> (He)'s (AS) almost hot and cold. He seems to be able to go for a week with no sexual needs, then BAM, he's all over me and we have a good romp, and he's good for another few days. (NT female)

> I would like my wife to have sex more often and to be more adventurous. (AS male)

Relationship stability, or lack of, decreases the frequency of sex. Constantly looking at other women, but will never do more. (AS male)

I have a high sex drive. I want sex every single day no matter what. I never masturbate. I enjoy collecting porn in my computer and staring at large-breasted women, but I will not masturbate while doing this. (AS male)

I would like my wife to show more interest and initiate sex. (AS male)

My partner (AS) does not understand that I would feel more inclined to have sex with him if he would help around the house and converse with me. Instead he just insists on having sex almost every day and I am resentful of this. (NT female)

As for the sex itself. It is far superior to anything I've experienced before with an NT lover. (NT female)

Excited by her excitement. If she wasn't excited, I wouldn't be. (AS male)

Men and women cannot share the same experience in sex (due to different bodily sensations) so I like to find experiences that we can both share. It is interesting to see how she will react. (AS male)

Low frequency/non-existent sex

A previous study by Maxine Aston (2003) found that around 50 per cent of couples where one or both partners had AS had no sexual relationship whatsoever. This current study found that over 60 per cent of couples reported dissatisfaction with their sex lives.

There was a lot of sadness and dissatisfaction with sexual issues in many of the relationships of those who completed the study. Many women felt unhappy about the little or no sex that their AS partners required, or alternatively felt resentful of the high sexual demands made by some partners. Some AS men were also unhappy about the expectations placed upon them to perform, the knowledge that they were unable to 'get it right' for their partners or that their partners were not meeting their high sexual needs. Some NT women had resigned themselves to very infrequent sex but still felt committed to the relationship. Some only had sex once or twice a year; or not at all for many years. These people felt that other areas of the relationship were great – shared interests, stability of the AS partner and friendship – and these made it acceptable for them:

> When I became pregnant 20 years ago, my AS spouse decided against having sex during my pregnancy because he didn't want to jostle the baby. Our sexual relationship never got back on track. I have had to be involuntarily without sex for the past 15 years with my partner. (NT female)

> He expressed to me that 'the honeymoon was over' and that sex was boring doing the same thing again and again. Also discussions about our sexual relating used to make him either confused, fitfully angry, frozen-up or scathing/ridiculing... I realised that I'd have to keep it to myself. (NT female)

> We are like room mates right now. (NT female)

> I have been for the last ten years in a loveless marriage. I stayed to keep three kids in their home that we ended up selling last year as my AS spouse lost his job and has not worked since. (NT female)

> We have always had trouble with our sexual relationship because he (AS) does not seen to have a strong desire for me sexually. (NT female)

> We both get too tired. He (AS) doesn't initiate sex often. Weeks can go by up to a couple of months. (NT female)

> My only sexual relationship is with my wife – and even then, sex is almost non-existent. (AS male)

No initiating with spouse in three years. (AS male)

What we want doesn't really match. (NT female)

He (AS) will have sex if he wants to and not if he doesn't whereas I would even if he wanted to often and even if I wasn't keen. Sometimes you can for the sake of the other's pleasure. (NT female)

There is currently some frustration on my part over the lack of sex in our marriage… I am hesitant about initiating intimacy because I do not want to come on too strong with my wife, being unsure about what she wants and having difficulty bringing it up with her. (AS male)

We have many strong bonds outside sex. These are what keep me here. I think my partner is fine with our relationship and can't realise that it's got a rather large unhealthy gap for me. (NT female)

For about the last 15 years we essentially haven't lived as man and wife sexually. This has not been healthy for me. (NT female with AS male partner)

I find it very sad that we cannot have a full sex life and I think it is so long since he (AS) had one that he does not miss it. (NT female)

He (AS) takes care of me, and he does his utmost to let me have or do anything I want. He accepts me, for who I am, and I love him for that, and I love him deeply. (NT female)

I do not have sex frequently; it is more effort than reward lately. (NT female)

We have had sex only five to six times a year for the past two to three years now. Outside of sex I feel we have a very good relationship. (NT female)

We only have sex about once every six to eight months. His excuse is always 'stress'. (NT female)

I'm pretty much in a non-sexual relationship now. I only try because she wants it and is getting upset that our relationship is not normal. I should never have married. I actually prefer to be alone, and being married makes me feel smothered. (AS male)

I've made my peace with it (lack of satisfactory sex) because he (AS) is a wonderful man and I don't believe he does any of this on purpose. I've really tried to change things over the years, and now I realise that it is not going to change. (NT female)

Difficulties in the bedroom

A small number of individuals reported specific issues that caused problems for them in their sexual relationships. These were sometimes physical difficulties or emotional issues preventing couples from maintaining a satisfactory sexual life together:

He (AS) has always needed me to help him find where to penetrate me during intercourse. (NT female)

I feel like I can not initiate for fear of rejection, so I don't. (NT female)

Whereas a normal couple would probably get comfortable/safe after a few years to try adventurous things, my AS uptightness has pretty much killed the likelihood of anything like that happening. (AS male)

When we have sex, I rarely have an orgasm. There is no one to blame here for this but it doesn't help that penetration lasts one to two minutes at most. He (AS) never asks for or talks about oral sex. (NT female)

Sexually speaking, our relationship has always been a wreck. (NT female)

I don't really enjoy sex with my husband (AS). I can't because he is so perfunctory about it. (NT female)

He (AS) wants to have sex, desperately. He just can't maintain an erection very long. I know he feels emasculated by this. (NT female)

He (AS) was a bit clumsy and unable to penetrate easily when other partners have just slipped into me unassisted. (NT female)

His (AS) erections were never quite firm enough to slide into my vagina on their own. Also he would have difficulty with sustaining the physical leg movement and strength required for him to reach orgasm; he would tire or say his legs hurt. (NT female)

She wants to have sex. She wants someone who worries when she is sick and a bunch of other touchy feely stuff that I can't do. (AS male)

Sex and stress

For some, sex becomes out of the question when other stressful situations arise but, for others, stress acts as a stimulant, increasing their libido and desire for sex. It is useful to monitor your own reactions to stress and external concerns to see what effect these may have on your sex drive:

I use sex as an emotional release, so if I'm stressed I want sex more often. (AS female)

I have a stronger sex drive when I am relaxed. In stressful situations I feel like I have to give my full attention to the cause of the stress rather than to my own sexual urges. (AS male)

I get over-stimulated easily when stressed or overly tired and that can change what I enjoy. (AS male)

If there is something I feel needs to get done and sex is 'getting in the way' of getting that higher priority thing done. If that situation comes up, I will not feel like I give in that way and try to flee if I think someone is trying to be sexual in a way with me that I cannot be at the time in question. (AS male)

Stress can certainly affect my sex drive. It actually fuels it at times. (AS male)

I use sex as a stress relief mechanism. My sex drive is rarely affected negatively by anything. (AS male)

I can't/don't want to perform if I am dissatisfied with the relationship at that time – I do not find sex as a solution to solve difficulties with the relationship. (AS male)

I can be troubled by external factors to the extent of it influencing my desire to be sexual. Sex tends to be a thing that's done only when my head is calm. When disturbed I become too self-centric – too much so to be interested in sex. (AS male)

My husband's (AS) sexual needs are tied to his stress level. The more stressed, the more sex he needs and the less likely he will be a considerate lover. (NT female)

My head just swims trying to read their response, and the result is that I can't maintain an erection, which of course makes it worse. (AS male)

Sexual preferences

Some of the respondents shared intimate thoughts about their sexual preferences and practices. Again, these are all personal and individual feelings and experiences, and it is not expected that everyone will have the same:

I'm a sexual omnivore. I enjoy anal as well as oral sex. Fucking doggy style is the most reliable way for me to come. The longer the lead-up time I have, the stronger the orgasm will be. (AS male)

It was hard to read his expressions or feel an intense connection at first… It seemed he was being purposefully distant and vague, even as we had intercourse. (NT female)

It is hard for me to describe the things that I find most pleasurable since when feelings are that intense I tend to lose myself and I will not be aware of exactly what my partner is doing to cause such intense feeling in me. (AS female)

Prefer to do action (sexual foreplay) than receive. (AS male)

My husband (AS) has an interest in the bondage and kink community. I am often forced into a position where he wants my blessing to attend an event where strangers will be naked… I know he would not engage in any sexual activity like touching, kissing… However, he would like me to give some kind of permission…either being tied up by someone or tying someone up. I struggle with this because in my mind these kinds of activities are sexual in nature… He would never fuck anyone else but he doesn't understand how I can't separate this in my mind. (NT female)

Only felt real with sex when relations are still innocent. After disturbances, arguments, fights etc. had started in the relationships, I lost any real heart for it at all. Just went through the motions from then on. Never felt as if I had any rights to the partner's body, or to the 'use' of the same. (AS male)

He (AS) refuses oral sex for me but he likes it for him. (NT female)

We like to be close, as much body contact as possible, and always naked when have sex. The length of time and the pace varies – sometimes fast and furious, other times more leisurely and we chat and laugh as we make love. It is often wonderfully moving and the most complete way that I feel he demonstrates his love for me. These are the times that I feel that I see the real him, not the person who has to pretend to fit in to the social world outside. (NT female)

8

Gender Identity
and Sexuality

When reading information about gender and sexuality in the autistic community, one often finds mention of some widely held beliefs that there is a difference in the way that some people view this area of their lives. There is mention of higher numbers of lesbian, gay, bisexual and transgender individuals within this population (Hénault 2006; Lawson 2005) and a sense of not being bound by gender in the same way that neuro-typical (NT) people are. This study found some evidence of ambiguity in sexuality and self-perception of gender in both Asperger Syndrome (AS) and NT responses.

Possible reasons for this reported difference may be:

- Gender can be viewed as a social construct (other than biological gender: 'male' and 'female'), which is embedded by interaction with same-sex peers and same-sex role models. If one has few or no peer relationships, it may be that this sense of gender – 'masculinity' and 'femininity' – is not as firmly established or perceived as relevant. The NT sense of who we are is often defined by the social groups we belong to and these messages are hard-wired through feedback – both positive and negative – from others.

- A self-centric perspective may mean that the idea of 'self in comparison to others' does not take place to the same extent, and a person with AS may not seek to fit into accepted norms of gender behaviour nor label themselves according to their gender.

- Some with AS may choose partners based on logical, practical reasons, such as sharing interests, rather than emotional attraction – a partner of either sex may fit this profile equally effectively for some people. In the majority of relationships, gender will be the primary consideration when selecting a partner.

- A person with AS who has had disappointing or rejecting encounters with those of the opposite sex may conclude that same-sex relationships may meet their needs better.

- Approval and societal expectations may not be a high priority – either because they are not understood or they are discarded; the meeting of an individual's own needs may override these considerations.

Women with AS – tomboys?

Writing and research on women with AS seem to show a tendency towards tomboyism and male-type behaviour. The heterosexual women with AS who responded to our questions were all in relationships with men with AS, who may particularly appreciate their (potentially) less emotionally demanding, more logical minds. One female NT/AS couple responded to the questionnaire and the AS partner was the more 'male' partner of the partnership.

There seems to be little need to conform and be part of a group in terms of wearing fashionable clothes and make-up for some women with AS. One woman found NT women 'stupid and annoying', and felt that she always offended them because she was unable to talk about the 'girlie' things they were interested in (personal communication, 2006).

Temple Grandin, the writer and scientist with high-functioning autism, describes how when growing up she noticed how other girls squealed when seeing the Beatles on TV. She thought they were cute but she wasn't going to behave in such a way just because of that. Temple went on to describe how she wasn't interested in the things that other girls enjoyed, such as make-up, clothes and jewellery, and how she preferred wood work. She perceived that boys had more fun and describes herself as a tomboy (personal communication, 2007). Temple also has a preference for male clothing, wearing cowboy shirts and jeans every day, because she finds them comfortable and practical.

In a comprehensive study of women with autistic spectrum conditions (Ingudomnukul *et al.* 2007), researchers found higher levels of testosterone, which contributed to a higher rate of certain medical conditions such as irregular periods, severe acne, polycystic ovary syndrome and hormone irregularities. Women in that study showed more tomboyish behaviour than the NT female control group. There was a greater likelihood of bisexuality and lower sexual interest in the AS women. The study showed that 17 per cent of the AS women considered themselves either asexual or having no preference for either sex. Whether this asexuality was a result of biological, social difficulties or other consequences is unclear.

Individuals with AS tend to display an extreme male profile – they perform better on systemising tests and poorer on empathising tests than NT individuals (Baron-Cohen 2003). Most of these studies have been carried out on men with AS, but those that have included women with AS show they have similar profiles:

> I usually tell people that I'm very tomboyish even now. I don't tend to do the typical things other females do. I do, however, do some things a typical male would do. (AS female)

Wendy Lawson, a gay female writer with an autistic spectrum condition, prefers to wear men's clothing because she says that it fits better than women's, is cheaper and better made. She also confirms that she was a tomboy as a child:

> I didn't 'feel' feminine, and most of the female roles expected of me I was uncomfortable with. (Lawson 2005)

After marriage and having children with a man, Wendy has come to terms with her sexuality later in life and is now openly gay and in a long-term relationship with a woman. Wendy describes a childhood of boyish pursuits – climbing trees and keeping lizards and of not feeling like a woman inside. She tried to make herself feel feminine by growing her hair long and wearing dresses. Wendy states that she feels more male than female and has come to feel comfortable with that in herself. Many women with AS prefer the company of boys/males to girls/women because they seem to be more interesting. Wendy married a man with a wonderful motorbike, despite not being sexually attracted to males at all. They remained married for 20 years before she was able to 'come out' autistically and sexually.

It is important for everyone to be able to accept themselves, whatever their sexuality. Reaching a place of self-acceptance, where you no longer try to pretend to yourself that you are something you're not, can be a great relief. This may be harder for family and friends to come to terms with because it may be a shock for them. Finding enjoyment from those of the same, different or both genders is legally acceptable if all are con-senting adults. Society may have prevailing views that are different from your own, and which may cause negative reactions in others. Deciding who to disclose sexual information to is a personal choice and may need some support from other people before reaching a conclusion.

Men with AS – less 'macho'?

One of the overriding characteristics that many women identify in their male AS partners is one of gentleness. Gender roles in these relationships are also often atypical, with the female partner taking on traditionally male roles and leading the decision making. Those with AS can be passive, which is a stereotypical female trait. Their preference for quiet, solitude and lack of interest in physical activities and team sports may give the impression of being less masculine, although the brain profile suggested by the 'extreme male brain' theory research (Baron-Cohen 2003) is one of overt maleness in its logical and systemising nature. Many men said that they had been presumed homosexual because of a lack of girlfriends, a tendency to spend time with females and being perceived as different from their male peers. Trying to be something you are not is rarely convincing and often too hard to keep up. Waiting to find someone who loves your qualities is a far more satisfactory way of living life:

I am so sensitive about my heterosexuality that I occasionally make inconspicuous comments about my desires for female companionship so as to avoid people thinking that I might be gay… I know I am definitely straight (even with this explanation, I feel the need to be defensive on the subject). (AS male)

It was probably cluelessness and lack of a partner that had me dancing suggestively like a woman in front of many people. (AS male)

I have always loved this about him (AS). On the one hand he lifts weights and has a big, beefy build, but on the other hand he is an ecologist and gets very excited about the first spring flowers. (NT female)

He (AS) used to bake me gingerbread and bring it in little carefully wrapped parcels… I was bemused and slightly suspicious of this effeminate loner who baked. (NT female)

My AS partner sometimes tries to attract my attention by using sexual posturing which is distinctly feminine. He flickers eyelids, puckers lips and holds his body in a way that makes him seem smaller and demure… This all struck me as a little odd at first. (NT female)

Sense of masculinity/femininity as a social construct

Respondents were asked how they viewed themselves in terms of gender because the author has experienced several people with AS who have expressed a lack of identity as a 'man' or 'woman' in a social sense and had difficulty understanding notions of masculinity and femininity. This is very much a social construct so, if one is less connected socially through a small or non-existent network and also less concerned with acceptance on any terms, these concepts may not be as firmly entrenched as for the socially orientated NT. Around 50 per cent of those asked stated that they either saw themselves and others as genderless or had no interest in expectations of males within society.

Although not asked, it is expected that many NTs see themselves clearly in terms of gender, and that this is a result of successful peer relationships and viewing one's self as part of a wider group, which they seek to fit into. Fitting into gender 'norms' in terms of appearance and behaviour is part of the requirements for social inclusion and acceptance; failure to do so marks an individual out as outside the group. This may be just another way that the individualist with AS is excluded from wider society, but the question must be asked: Would you want to be part of such a narrowly defined majority that excludes on the basis of what it classifies as 'male/female' behaviour?

> I'm just a person. I know of no distinction between the sexes other than the physical. (AS male)

> I never use the word 'man' or 'male' in reference to myself, unless it is required of me... Instead I think of myself as 'what I am'. (AS male)

> I did for a time see myself in the third person. Steven this and Steven that. (AS male)

> I have said for years that I've never seen or experienced myself as a male, always have seen myself as a 'person'. Have described myself as having the male 'urge' but not the male 'instinct' if you can see the difference. (AS male)

> I never gave a damn for what 'a man' is supposed to be, didn't give a damn for mere social conventions. They didn't apply to me. (AS male)

> I never had a sense of myself as a man until I was 54 and in therapy. I had only ever experienced the world as filled with 'people'. (AS male)

> He (AS) does not like the expectations that society puts on men. (NT female)

> I believe myself to be just a person. (AS female)

I don't know that I see myself as male or female... I do know that I see all other people as genderless first. (AS male)

I resent gender roles and other stereotypes, and regard myself (and prefer to be regarded) as a unique individual. (AS male)

I do not fit the classic male role; I am slightly more androgynous than the norm. On a scale, 1 being female, 5 being neutral and 10 being male, I rate myself a 7. (AS male)

I do know that I see all other people as genderless first. (AS male)

As a child, teen and in early adulthood I thought I should have been born a man. It is possible that I have a male spirit in a female body...but I am OK with that now. (AS female)

I have always had trouble fitting into the stereotypically feminine role. I used to really want to feel comfortable conforming to that ideal. Now I am happy closer to androgyny. I am what I am, just like Popeye. (NT with 'strong AS traits' female)

I have no sense of what it means to be a man, as opposed to a person. (AS male)

Bisexuality and sexual confusion

Of the NT women who answered, several had had relationships or experiences with women prior to their relationship with their male AS partner, but none considered themselves to be bisexual now. Perhaps there is something about men with AS that is appealing in a less macho way, or perhaps women who are less rigid about their own societal roles have a greater acceptance and attraction for men who are also discarding rigid notions of 'expected' roles and behaviour. More research needs to be carried out in this area to determine whether there is any real difference between AS and NT perspectives and behaviour in this area.

Of the women with AS, three out of four were either bisexual or gay, representing 75 per cent of the (small) sample. This is a high proportion despite the size of the sample, and may reflect a more open approach to sexuality by some women with AS and less need to adhere to social norms or peer expectations. A small number of the men with AS who responded (8%) reported either bisexuality or some confusion with regard to their sexuality in the past, with the remaining men with AS stating that they had experienced no doubt as to their heterosexuality:

> I had wondered what it might be like to be a woman…the reason that I have wondered about being female is that it might simply be easier to make friends and form relationships. (AS male)

> I have experienced some confusion… Some years ago I felt curiosity about experimenting with the same sex but never acted upon it. (AS male)

> I've sometimes wondered what it is like from the woman's perspective. I'd love to try it out for a month or so, but in the end I prefer to be a man. (AS male)

> He (AS) is sometimes turned on by the male body when he's taking ecstasy (drug) but this always translates into an enhanced desire to be with a female. (NT female)

> I am attracted to both genders but have only had relationships and sexual experiences with men. (AS female)

> Some (confusion) in my youth. I would imagine myself as a woman and about experiencing sex as a woman. (AS male)

> Inside my body I didn't feel like a woman, whatever that is meant to be. (NT female)

> When I was young I was pretty flat-chested. I easily passed for a male youth. Whenever someone called me son I felt pleased and at home. (NT female)

> For some time he (AS) was confused, he got many books on the topic, then decided he liked girls better. (NT female)

At college he (AS) said he felt in love with a male classmate or if not fully in love, he was strongly attracted to him. (NT female)

I am bisexual so I enjoy sex with people of both genders. I do prefer men, but women are enjoyable as well, and do turn me on. (AS female)

My AS spouse was bisexual before our marriage. I did not find that out until years later. He blamed it on cocaine use. (NT female)

Previous research suggests that men with AS who had homosexual relationships outside their primary heterosexual relationship did so purely for sexual reasons (Aston 2003). These men found it easier to have this sexual arrangement than to have sex with their female partners, who could demand more emotional closeness than other men. These men had no sexual relationships at all with their female partners, who accepted this. These men did not see themselves as homosexual and had no preference for men as partners, but purely as a manageable form of sexual satisfaction. It seems then that a small number of those with AS do not see biological sex as the first consideration when selecting a partner, and may choose someone for other reasons.

Hénault (2006) reports instances of transvestism where men with AS seek to look and be like women in order to gain acceptance from them. They may have experienced care from women and want to be part of that group. There is no evidence that cross-dressing indicates homosexuality or a desire to be a woman.

Friendships with the opposite sex

Several of those questioned expressed a preference for the company of the opposite sex for friendships. It may be that neither men nor women with AS 'fit' with their own same-sex peers and find these relationships difficult. Women perhaps don't feel sexually threatened by AS men due to their less overtly macho nature and may feel a need to nurture them. AS women often find NT women illogical and more interested in talking about emotional issues than sharing knowledge, and so may seek the less intimate nature of male friendships. Accepting that one prefers the company of the opposite sex can be a relief, rather than continuing to try to establish relationships with those who do not interest you socially:

> I love the company of women, for talk, I love talking sex with them regardless of whether I have any relations with them at all. (AS male)

> Always took it for granted that I could get on well with women. Always have had great friendships with women. (AS male)

> In social settings (he) (AS) prefers to be where the women are chatting. (NT female)

> I always have my antennae out for intimacy and female closeness and will greedily move in on any woman who feels promising. (AS male)

> I've always liked female company and never male company. Women do emotions better than men, men are boring competitive and you can't shag them, so they're really uninteresting compared to women! (AS male)

> (The) babysitter is 12 years younger than me, but my mental/emotional maturity is about the same as hers so I get along very well with her. (AS male)

> I find that I prefer the company of women and have been told that I am an 'honorary girly' and have a strong feminine side. (AS male)

9

Infidelity and Inappropriate Behaviour

For some people with Asperger Syndrome (AS) (and without), the boundaries of a relationship are different from those that would be perceived as typical.

Often having a strong dislike for authority, demands made upon them and being told what to do, a person with AS can react strongly to reasonable expectations of behaviour from a long-term partner. The person may place demands and boundaries on their partner but object to similar requests being made on them. It is necessary to recognise that there are rules for relationships. These rules will be different for each couple and need to be negotiated and explicitly stated. This is especially the case in AS relationships because these rules may not be naturally understood. Both parties need to understand what is acceptable to their partner and what is not, in order to prevent friction and disagreement. If either party finds the boundaries placed upon the relationship unacceptable, they are entitled to disagree and ultimately to leave the relationship:

> I think things can get difficult when and if one isn't familiar with the 'rules' or if the goalposts move and the rules change. I also think relationships can be problematic if they are not grounded in mutual understanding, autonomy and respect (AS female). (Lawson 2005, p.15)

Inappropriate relationships and flirting

Several people responded that their friendships, relationships and behaviour towards others had caused difficulties with their partners. Previous research states that some neuro-typical (NT) women describe their partners with AS as flirts (Aston 2003). The inability to express and interpret communication signals and messages appropriately may cause this assumption. There may also be an extreme desire to be accepted and liked, stemming from a lifetime of being poorly received and rejected. When confronted, the person with AS will appear surprised that their actions have been misinterpreted in this way and cannot understand why their partner is upset:

> When speaking to other women, even when buying something in a shop, he (AS) appears over-friendly and flirtatious, calling them by their first name (if on a name badge) and almost ignoring me. I am sure this is not paranoia on my part. When I have said this to him, he looks amazed and assures me that he was just talking. The whole concept of knowing how to flirt is completely alien to him and I don't believe he is capable – certainly doing it in front of your girlfriend is not the best tactic! I don't get upset by it because I know he has had such a rough time getting on with anyone and that he would never mean to hurt me. (NT female)

The concept of flirting and engaging in subtle communication signals is a sophisticated art, which can be difficult for those with AS to master successfully due to their condition. It involves being able to read indirect and non-verbal signals from others as to their interest and availability, predict behaviour, engage in small talk and also to express one's own interest subtly and non-verbally. This sounds like an AS minefield!

> My wife was upset that I continued to correspond with an old friend of mine (female) after they had a falling out. I have so few friends who correspond with me that it was annoying to have to give up one of my last friends. (AS male)

> Well that happened more than once (partner had sex with someone else while in the marriage). Betrayal, a trust issue,

anger and resentment. The beginning of the end of an 18-year marriage. (NT female)

There have been two occasions. We split up one day and he (AS) was having sexual phone calls from an ex-partner the next day. He felt that we were not together so he could do what he liked and could not understand why I was upset. He was also in another relationship yet told me he loved me regularly. This partner did not want him to have contact with me, but he still did. (NT female)

I had two women friends who I did not introduce to my wife (but was very open about). She was very agitated about these and I steadfastly refused to accept that she should 'vet' these relationships. They were MY private relationships. She could trust me, or hurt: it was her choice. I really consciously pushed the envelope here... At the same time, I never really believed the relationship would/could break. How socially stupid is that? Not so much mind-blind but consequence blind. (AS male)

She (NT) accused me of having affairs all the time even though I wasn't. I can be cuddly with people that I shouldn't be. I don't back off if they come towards me as I fear upsetting them if I move away. (AS male)

My current partner is very possessive and demands to know if I have any contact of any sort with previous partners. She knows I have no friends for me to come into contact with, or be led astray by. (AS male)

I had an affair with a co-worker...which almost broke up my marriage. I enjoy attention from all ladies and my wife gets angry about this. (AS male)

I did this (had sex with someone else while married) twice – with her knowledge around 20–25 years ago. Despite the hurt and fear (that I would leave – something I never

> thought of for a single moment in 34 years...), she stayed in the relationship for the long term. (AS male)

> I did have an affair once with a woman I met at work but talked with on the internet. I eventually broke up with her and went back to my wife. (AS male)

There seems to be some evidence that those with AS who do behave inappropriately generally have no intent to cause harm or pain. The person may be operating under a different set of rules and logic. As it is accepted that those with AS have a different means of processing in other areas of life, it would be naïve to expect that this wouldn't also have an effect within sexual and personal relationships. Unfortunately, this is one of the most emotive and sensitive topics of all and, when people feel wronged in an intimate sense, their reactions tend to be highly emotionally charged and potentially confusing for the person with AS. Maxine Aston (2003) found that AS partners who had sexual relationships outside their main relationship viewed the matter objectively and without the emotions that would be expected by an NT partner, such as guilt or remorse:

> My (AS) partner would have sex with me in my sleep. If I woke up he would tell me that I had initiated it and woken him up! No other partner in my life has ever said that I have done this so I'm sure it's not me, but it did make me confused and wonder if I had gone mad. (NT female)

Infidelity

There may also be a tendency to compartmentalise sex as separate from any kind of emotional connection, as discussed earlier. This is commonly believed to be more typical of males than females within the general population, but it also appears to exist in the AS population. This viewpoint from AS males and some AS females may explain how difficulties in relationships can occur. If the AS partner does not feel that having sex with another person constitutes an act of betrayal or infidelity because for them there is a clear distinction between loving a partner and having sex, problems can arise.

When asked what constituted infidelity, the general trend was that, for NT partners, intent, emotional closeness and flirting were as much a sign of betrayal as physical contact – all were seen as inappropriate behaviour. For those with AS, some felt that penetration was the only mark of infidelity – perhaps taking the term literally. Others seemed to be more concerned with their partner sharing emotional closeness and were less concerned as to whether they were having sex with someone else. Two couples felt that sex with another person was acceptable if it had been agreed first. These couples consisted of both partners having AS. Only one NT woman felt that it might be OK for their partner to have sex with someone else, but only if it was mutually agreed beforehand:

> Intimacy is more intellectual than physical. Sharing hopes and dreams with someone else can be infidelity. (AS male)

> He (AS) does not see how holding another person's hand could be infidelity. He wanted scenarios! (NT female)

> (He) (AS) can be very sexy and flirtatious without realising it… This relentless desire to impress around females can sometimes come off as a message if wanting something more… Now that we're in a committed relationship…he immediately tells women that he's attached and becomes almost aloof around them. (NT female)

> I haven't really thought about this (infidelity). I guess deep kissing, fondling, penetration. It's not a big issue with me. (AS male)

> I'd understand why (the concept of my partner having sex with someone else). I'd only feel hurt because she'd believe she was hurting me. (AS male)

> Strictly speaking, in the long run, sexual infidelity for me is nowhere near as serious a breach of trust as a personal attack or verbal abuse and a violent squabble, regardless of the absence of physical abuse. (AS male)

> It's done. I'm outta here (or if they imported their things into my place it's they're outta here)! (AS male)

Other than the risk of sexually transmitted diseases, I do not see why I would have an issue with it. (AS male)

Sex is just part of a relationship, not the whole thing. Ultimately, I think my feelings on this matter (infidelity) can be summed up by the question: who is she 'with' (who is she having a relationship with)? And if the answer is me, then I'm satisfied. (AS male)

If it was done above board and we'd discussed it beforehand, I could accept it. I would worry that he'd like the other person more than me, especially at first. ('AS traits' female)

I would have a retaliatory affair to 'teach her a lesson' if she had sex with another person while with me. (AS male)

I'd want to know why it happened and what it meant to our relationship. I guess I'd feel confused. (AS male)

I would definitely consider holding hands or anything more to be infidelity. (AS male)

If she would ever want to be very close with other men, I would feel I've lost her. I would reluctantly allow such infidelity if she were to tell me that she is just experimenting with different men to find her soul mate. Although this would make me fearful of STDs (sexually transmitted diseases) if we are sexually active. (AS male)

If it was arranged beforehand and he talked to me about it both before and after...no problem. (AS female)

I would regard it as dangerous and risky rather than as immoral or insulting. (AS male)

(I) would feel sure that I must have let her down. Would be so very aware that the other person must be NT and have all the capabilities and 'normal' reactions and styles that I lack as an Aspie. (AS male)

The determination is intent. If the partner feels the need to hide these actions then it is likely that they are doing something that could be defined as cheating. (AS female)

Depends if it (sex with another person) was negotiated or not. (AS female)

The relationship would be over. Divorce is necessary. (AS male)

Anything with another person that involves more than a platonic relationship. If anyone could look and get the wrong idea, then it is infidelity. (AS male)

Betrayal and then hatred. (Asked: What would your feelings be if your partner had sex with another person while in a relationship with you?) (AS male)

I have always kept in touch with ex-girlfriends and sometimes my current partners want to know why… It makes me angry and I refuse to be 'bullied' like this. I don't see why being in a relationship means I should have any friendships proscribed. (AS male)

Intellectually, I regard imposing restrictions on one's partner to be acts not of love but of possessiveness. Whether I would act according to my ideals, I don't know due to lack of experience. (AS male)

He (AS) would be OK with me having sex with another woman if he could watch. He doesn't however want to participate. (NT female)

Monogamous, but with room for play. (AS male)

(Had sex with another person) When I was having sex with someone who saw it as more of a relationship than I did. (AS male)

If she has a secret 'love triangle', I would quickly turn it into a 'love line segment'. The end points of that segment would be her and her other partner, while I would be a lonely point on the plane once more. (AS male)

Sometimes I feel like having an outside relationship but I won't. It is just that I want to feel like someone is keen on me and someone wants to be close. (NT female)

Sexual offences

There are some reports that those with AS can be involved in obsessive behaviour relating to individuals such as stalking and harassment. There has been some media interest in making a link between the person's AS and their offence, although these individuals comprise a small minority of those with AS. None of those questioned had experience of this type of behaviour, but since most were, or had been, in a relationship, this suggests that this would be less likely. Reasons for engaging in harassment can be a genuine lack of understanding of social signals by the person with AS. The focus of their attention may have been kind of friendly and this may have been misinterpreted. There may be a difficulty in perceiving that upset or distress is being felt by the person due to less mature 'theory of mind' abilities. There will doubtless be a logical thought process that has occurred in the mind of the person with AS, which has resulted in the behaviour. It is unlikely that there is real understanding of the consequences of the behaviour for themselves or their target:

I can't read sexual signals easily and this has got me into trouble before as I've often thought that people were being friendly when they were coming on to me sexually, and this has hurt and upset my partner greatly. (AS male)

I have now refused to put myself in a vulnerable position in the bedroom because I don't think he (AS) can control himself and respect my boundaries. (NT female)

For some people with AS, sex can become an overriding fascination and obsession. Hénault (2006) suggests a list of questions to ask an individual with AS who seems to be exhibiting excessive sexual interest:

- What sexual behaviours are involved?

- How long has the obsession been present?

- Under what circumstances does the obsession express itself (time of day, preceding and following activities, and individuals involved)?

- What purpose does the obsession serve?

- How does the individual behave when he or she talks about the obsession?

- What emotions accompany the repetitive behaviour(s): anxiety, anger, sadness, fear, joy, excitement?

The answers to these questions may help to outline the function of the obsessive behaviour and provide some potential approaches for support. It may be that sexual gratification is the sole source of pleasure and excitement in the individual's life. The behaviour may decrease anxiety or stimulate sensory senses for the individual (Hénault 2006). Like any other strong fascination of the person with AS, there may be a sense of control and accomplishment in being an 'expert' in something – it may simply be another passing interest, which is enhanced by the sensitive and taboo nature of the topic:

> I am really obsessed with sex. I think about it all the time and would love to do it every day. My wife gets mad at me for talking about it all the time. (AS male)

> Infatuation with woman at work got me fired. (AS male)

The inability to read communication could, at its most serious, result in someone with AS forcing themselves on to someone whom they believe is a willing partner, only to discover that this is not the case. This could potentially lead to accusations of sexual assault or rape (Aston 2003). It is important that the person with AS ensures that they have received a clear indication that sexual advances are welcomed before acting. There are some reports of sexually inappropriate behaviour from people with AS and these seem to be more likely to be a misunderstanding of the rules rather than a deliberate attempt to harm or upset anyone.

Tony Attwood (2006) reports that he has encountered individuals with AS who have committed offences of a sexual nature, often due to an obsession or infatuation with a person, or as the result of inappropriate behaviour. The person may not understand that their feelings are not reciprocated, nor realise that their attention is unwanted. There may be an inappropriate, socially unacceptable sexual attachment to specific items or people – children, animals or objects, which can cause the person to come to the attention of the authorities. Sexual offending isn't more common within the AS population, but it may be a result of the expression and experience of having AS (Hénault 2006). Lack of typical adolescent sexual encounters, difficulty reading and expressing non-verbal signals and emotional feelings, and tending to follow one's own path may all be factors. It has been suggested that Jeffrey Dahmer, a sexual serial killer, had AS (Silva *et al.* in Hénault 2006).

A fascination with pornography may cause difficulties if the person is unable to contain the viewing of the material to the privacy of their home. One man with AS who responded to the survey had been fired from his job for viewing pornography at his workplace. If this had been an establishment involving children or other vulnerable groups, this could have led to arrest. The desire to meet one's needs may override the person's perception of the appropriateness of the behaviour. It may also be difficult for a person with AS to transfer the concept that looking at pornography is OK in one setting but not in another. Less developed empathy/'Theory of Mind' skills may mean that the individual is not able to appreciate the consequences of their behaviour on others, making their own needs the only consideration. The tendency to speak the truth can also result in a person with AS making inappropriate remarks to others, which may be taken as offensive when the person only intends to express their thoughts or opinions.

In most situations, it appears that deliberate intent to harm is not generally the case in offences committed by those with AS, but that they may be perceiving the world in a different way with different understandings and drives. Information and guidance may help to prevent inadvertent criminality and arrest. There is no evidence to suggest that those with AS are more likely to commit sexual offences.

10

Great Sex!

What makes a good sexual relationship?

To sum up: great communication seems to equal great sex. Acceptance, understanding, talking and listening appear to be the keys to a good relationship and, consequently, a good sex life. It is stated (Aston 2003; Attwood 2006) that the requisites for a successful Asperger Syndrome (AS) relationship are acknowledgement of the existence of AS by both partners, a willingness to learn and change by both partners, and a willingness to access and implement specialist AS information from counselling services, literature or other support means. The appreciation that often the partner with AS is doing the best they can, as much as they can and in the only way they can, is useful to remember. Criticism, negativity and feelings of failure tend not to enhance anyone's desire for intimacy and sex, AS or no AS. A sense of trust and safety is very important for a person with AS who may have had a huge number of negative experiences. The person who can offer this unconditional acceptance may benefit from a relaxed, loving, giving partner. This is not an easy task when the differences between partners can feel like a gulf, but the rewards may be great:

> My most important point is that once I became (his) wife, I was for all purpose his. He became comfortable with my persona, my body and my touch. I know this had not happened ever before and it was (and is) very important to me. I knew coming into this relationship that he had issues with letting people into his private space, but I just did not know it was called AS at first. (NT female)

We still have marital issues but our relationship is stronger than ever. Mostly because we BOTH are working on it. He tries his best and I have learned to give him credit for his 'baby steps' towards being a more involved partner. (NT female)

Of those questioned, many individuals and couples expressed dissatisfaction with their sexual relationships. Some neuro-typical (NT) partners felt that, if it wasn't for having such a good relationship outside the sexual side, they would no longer remain in the relationship. The overriding perception of the thoughts of AS partners was that they would remain in the relationship regardless of whether their sexual needs were met. This fits with a passivity that often comes with AS – a sense that the person has no responsibility, right or ability to make changes or demands. The imposition of demands from a partner can cause feelings of indignity: 'How dare they tell me what to do?' Control is a major issue for those with AS: trying to gain a hold on a complex and unpredictable world may not leave much room for compromise or meeting the needs of a partner. There may be a sense that, if these requests are met, more may follow and with them discomfort. Sometimes it may take time for a person with AS to accommodate someone else's needs. Responding emotionally and negatively – typical and understandable reactions to sensitive sexual matters – can make an AS partner terrified of making a mistake and never wanting to broach the subject again. Discussing these subjects calmly can allow the AS partner to understand clearly what is required of them. They simply may not know. They cannot guess.

What makes a couple happy sexually?

Among the couples questioned, those who were having satisfactory sex lives shared a number of characteristics: they all appreciated and accepted the positive facets of AS that their partner had. All the heterosexual AS/AS partnerships reported happy sex lives and so did those who, while not AS/AS couples, had lesser degrees of neuro-typicality in the non-AS partner – Attention Deficit Hyperactivity Disorder (ADHD), 'AS traits', dyslexia, etc. Temple Grandin says that the happiest couples she has seen within the AS community are those where the spouse is either AS or eccentric, and the findings from this small study seem to bear this out (Grandin 1996). Perhaps because the non-AS/NT partner views the world in a unique way, they are more able to appreciate the quirks and individuality of their partner with AS, or perhaps they actively seek an unusual person due to their own individuality. All the couples who claimed to have a rewarding sexual side to their relationship seemed to have a good understanding of AS and were willing and able to make adjustments to maintain low stress levels for their partners. They did not express resentment or anger about their partner's behaviour, but understanding and acceptance. This appears to be very important to those with AS: to be able to be themselves. The people who were able to do this enjoyed strong relationships with loyal and devoted partners, who were also able to perform sexually and appreciate their partners' needs.

We asked our respondents to describe the positive and special aspects of their sexual relationships with their partners with AS:

> What we have is so far above any other I've ever dreamt I'd know, or feel. (NT female)

> Other than learning more about what would turn us both on I can't think of anything that would make our love life better. (NT female)

> I want to get what I want out of this relationship. In order to do this I must make an effort. (AS male)

> I believe my sex life is better than the typical NT relationship. Neither of us uses it as a weapon or tool to get what we want. (AS female)

> I love being the only woman who's ever been able to get this close to him. (NT female)

> Sex is a binding part of a relationship for me. It shows acceptance of each other. The most joyous sensation that a couple can share is the same as the most horrific sensation a female can experience (rape). It shows a huge amount of trust for a female to allow that to happen. (AS male)

I felt he (AS) was in the moment with me and not off in a fantasy world. (NT female)

I almost prefer some of his AS ways of relating because to me they seem more genuine and meaningful. There's no manipulation. There's no use of my feelings to accomplish other motives. He never tells me he loves me if he doesn't mean it 100 per cent. (NT female)

I hope that I have taught (him) that there's nothing wrong with him and there's no reason to feel that he can't have a meaningful relationship with someone…he just has to find the 'right' person and help them understand. (NT female)

I plan to be with this man forever. (NT female)

I can honestly say that it was the most deeply meaningful sex of my life. (NT female)

He (AS) is more attentive to my needs, and pays close attention to what things turn me on and what I don't enjoy. (AS female)

The only positive relationship I've had is one that has had central to it the understanding, knowledge and acceptance of my AS. (AS male)

Low self-esteem has probably caused me to choose controlling, manipulative partners in the past. I have had two relationships with AS men who were not into mind games or not very good at them. It gives me a lot of peace. (NT female)

I can say without reservation that I trust my partner. I think AS is responsible for an honesty in word and deed, the like of which I do not find in NT relationships and society at large. It is the raw truth he speaks when he says he loves me. It's not a ploy. It's not to get something out of me. It's just his overwhelming feeling right at that moment. What's not to love here? (NT female)

He's the one lover I can say has truly made me feel alive and accepted in and out of bed. He has taken me to heights I never imagined before he touched me. (NT female)

I find him to be a very interesting lover, it is never the same twice... With my other partners it's always been boring, but with an AS partner you never quite know how you are going to make love, very unpredictable. (NT female)

No head games. No unrealistic expectations. No hard feelings. (AS male)

I certainly do not have to worry about not being attractive to my husband, because he constantly tells me I'm sexy and he wants to make love to me. (NT female)

I got to be his special interest for a few years. That was nice. He also made pleasing me sexually a priority, which I couldn't resist. He has a gentle and tender soul overall, which makes me feel safe. He gives me unconditional love, which I haven't gotten from anyone else in my life and don't seem to consistently be able to give back to him (to my shame)! (NT female)

I feel that I can trust him because of his AS. I've been hurt very badly in the past and it's taking time to trust anyone. (NT female)

I couldn't see going through life without knowing my husband, and I wouldn't want to go through it without his love. (NT female)

Does talking about sex help?

Those partners who expressed satisfaction with their sexual relationships appeared to understand that explicit communication was required and that, if provided, their partner with AS was often more than happy to meet those needs. There seemed to be a requirement for clear direction and instruction because the person was perhaps unable to guess what was desired by reading signals. Knowing what is expected may reduce anxiety for a partner who can be confident that they have a good chance of success, rather than fearing failure by misreading signals, upsetting their partner and being subject to criticism, which they may find very hard to take:

> I ask him what he needs and tell him it's OK to let me know in any way he can. (NT female)

> I try to listen to my partner. I try to satisfy my partner to the best of my ability. She says something, unless there is something I don't feel safe about, I try to see to it that her requests are honoured and respected, and carried out. (AS male)

> (He) displays a fabulous ability and willingness to meet my needs if I specify exactly what those needs are. (NT female)

> I have no inhibitions about asking him to 'be gentle' or 'go faster' or 'focus in' on me in bed, and he's happy to oblige anything I ask. That very fact carries a lot of value which more than 'pays for' the other 'deficiencies'. (NT female)

> I believe my AS partner understands me better that any of the NT partners I have had. (AS female)

> It is at times 'differently' frustrating and takes a great deal of listening, and going over what the 'context issue' is as opposed to the 'it's my fault, I'm not enough of this, too much of that'. (NT female)

> Since we have been learning about AS and talking about things, we have both been trying harder to gain a little more understanding for each other; our relationship has been improving to the point we had sex two times this week. (NT female)

Handy hints for good sexual relationships

- Take things slowly when you first meet someone. Think about how you will tell them about your AS. If you don't tell them, they will not understand why you communicate differently. It is unlikely that you will be able to hide it for long and you may get into a situation that you cannot handle. If someone cannot accept you for being yourself, they are probably not worth being with.

- Take time to listen and spend time doing activities that your partner likes to do.

- Ask questions about their day and remember details of their lives. This is seen as a demonstration that you care.

- Make an effort to be clean, look and smell nice – this is basic respect for another person.

- Be honest with a new partner about how much sexual experience you have had. Ask a partner to tell/show you how they like to be touched. Everyone is different and you cannot assume that what you like (or what a previous partner liked) will be the same for someone else.

- If you cannot speak honestly and openly with a sexual partner about sexual health and contraception, you shouldn't be having sex with them.

- An appreciation of the AS partner and their efforts is important, especially as they may experience low self-esteem and extensive stress and anxiety. Realising that some sensory issues may be causing severe discomfort, and trying to negotiate a compromise on physical touch, may be required.

- The AS partner can help by providing as much support and interest in their partner outside the bedroom. If a partner expresses that they don't enjoy seeing porn or being touched sexually during the day, it is important to respect this, regardless of your feelings on the subject. Ignoring a partner's requests is a sure way for them not to want sex. If a person feels angry or uncared for, they are unwilling to share intimacy with a partner.

- A willingness to accommodate the needs of both partners and understand that both partners have an equal right to satisfaction may be helpful. If the needs being requested are unpleasant or uncomfortable for either partner, they may be refused or negotiated.

- Sexual blackmail – 'If you won't do that for me, I won't do this for you' – does not inspire an atmosphere of love and willingness to please.

- Maintaining a low stress environment for the AS partner will make them more able to relax and enjoy pleasurable sex.

- Find an acceptable frequency of sexual activity for both partners. This will vary widely from more than once a day to once every few months. No one is wrong or 'abnormal': it's a personal choice.

- Sex does not have to mean penetration; oral or manual stimulation may satisfy a partner if not in the mood for intercourse. Sometimes a kiss and a cuddle is all that a partner needs to feel loved.

- Accommodate each other's needs – do things when not in the mood sometimes.

- Be open to persuasion. Allow your partner to put you in the mood when you may feel like saying 'no'. You never know, you might enjoy it!

- Showing an NT partner that they are cared for and supported will make them more willing to meet their partner's sexual needs. Ask them what they need help with.

- If a partner is unhappy with other aspects of life, they may be less likely to want sex. Sex is an emotional act as well as a physical one for many people, and the two are connected.

- Talking and listening about each other's sexual likes and dislikes can be helpful in improving sex.

- Understand that another person may find different sensations and activities pleasurable. Take the time to find out what these are.

- If your partner is happy and relaxed, they are more likely to want sex.

- Stress, over-work and anxiety are the most likely causes of reduced libido.

- Tell your partner regularly that you find them sexually attractive.

- Be aware that everyone's sexual appetite is different – if your partner wants more or less sex, that doesn't mean that they are 'wrong'. They are simply different, and a middle way needs to be found to meet all needs.

- Women, especially, often need to feel that they are valued and loved as a person, rather than seen as a sexual object. Taking the time to hold, kiss and listen to your partner will increase her willingness to have sex.

- If one partner is unhappy with the sexual relationship, this can cause the relationship to break down. If one partner has a problem, you both have a problem. Ignoring it will not make it go away.

- Do not expect your AS partner to 'know' whether you want sex or not. They may be unable to read the signals. Say explicitly what you want, or, if this feels uncomfortable, organise some signs between you that they can read to understand your feelings.

11

Conclusion

From the responses I have had, other research and publications that I have read (Aston 2003; Attwood 2002, 2006; Slater-Walker and Slater-Walker 2002; Stanford 2003) and my own experience (Hendrickx and Newton 2007), there is strong evidence that mutually satisfying personal and sexual relationships are happily occurring within the Asperger Syndrome (AS) population. It is also evident that some relationships have significant problems, which are resulting in one or both partners feeling unhappy and dissatisfied. I would like to think that these issues could be resolved with increased understanding and awareness from both partners, but I am also realistic enough to know that the motivation to be tolerant and understanding of long-standing resentments may be hard to muster. For some couples, it is simply too late: the knowledge of the existence of AS in their relationships did not come soon enough. Most of the couples who participated discovered AS later in life and well into their relationships. It is hoped that in the future, with earlier diagnosis, greater self-acceptance, and more knowledge and understanding from within the person's wider circle, that relationship issues will be more easily identified and discussed because the causes will be known.

The general picture suggests that, in general, males with AS have their first sexual experience later and have fewer sexual partners than their neuro-typical (NT) counterparts. The sample here consisted mostly of men with AS and has not been compared with a similar NT population, but in general terms that can be said to be the case. There are difficulties with the validity of any statistics involving personal and intimate topics because the word and memory of the participant has to be relied upon. Women with AS may be more at risk of sexual abuse and more vulnerable than their NT peers as a result of misreading signals and believing what they are told by potentially predatory partners. This group – although small in this sample – tended to have sex earlier and have as many, if not more, partners than many of their NT counterparts.

There is some evidence that sensory issues play a part in the sexual relationships of those with AS, whether as an enhancement to stimulation or as a hindrance to physical intimacy – especially in the case of noise, smell or tactile over-sensitivity. For some with AS, pornography and/or masturbation are preferred to sexual interaction with a partner due to the complex communication required to initiate and comprehend the needs of another person. This causes feelings of sadness and low self-esteem by those who feel rejected by this lack of interest from their partner with AS.

In our study, low self-esteem affected many people with AS in their willingness to attempt new relationships. Some people had been so affected by the breakdown of a relationship that they had remained alone for many years before attempting a new one. Others felt unable to engage in a relationship until later in life as a result of not believing themselves to be attractive or worthy of a partner.

Those who perceived their partner's AS as being the cause of their sexual difficulties were (unsurprisingly) having unhappy and unfulfilled relationships. This seemed to go hand in hand with a difficulty or unwill-ingness of the AS person to acknowledge and accept their differences from those of their partner. Communication seems to be key, and also a genuine trust that what the AS partner experiences is real and important to them. There was a sense from some partners that the AS person was being deliberately cruel and difficult, rather than an understanding that they communicated and interacted differently.

It is gratifying to hear that some people are having great sex and that others are enjoying their unattached status. Overwhelmingly, the picture from this small sample demonstrates that those who are the most content with their relationships and sex lives fit into a specific category. They are couples where either both partners have AS or one partner has AS and the other identifies themself as having 'AS traits' or other neuro-diversity of their own (dyslexia, Attention Deficit Disorder [ADD]). It seems that dif-ference attracts and accepts difference by merit of understanding another's unique take on the world. Often the non-AS partners came across as quite unusual people with a varied past prior to meeting their AS partner. These couples also both accepted and acknowledged AS and could see the special qualities and positive aspects that it brought to the relationship. They could recognise the limitations but did not focus on them in a negative sense. In comparing their current AS partner to previous NT partners sexually, the AS partner was described as being the more considerate and better lover. Sometimes this took some time and patience on the partner's part, but it was willingly given. There seems to be a sense of reframing the picture to see it as a good thing, and that maybe some people are better able to do this than others.

The key to satisfactory sex and a happy relationship appears to be acceptance, patience, understanding and an appreciation of the uniqueness of AS in a partner. The AS partner also needs to accept and acknowledge their differences, be willing to listen and learn from their partner and recognise that both parties have the right to have their desires satisfied. The environment necessary for that kind of communication is one of love, openness, trust and an understanding of reciprocity. If we can remember this in all our relationships, at all times, then potentially we can all find the life that suits our needs.

Accept, respect and enjoy.

References

Aston, M. (2003) *Asperger's in Love.* London: Jessica Kingsley Publishers.

Attwood, T. (2002) *Why Does Chris Do That?* London: National Autistic Society.

Attwood, T. (2006) *The Complete Guide to Asperger Syndrome.* London: Jessica Kingsley Publishers.

Baron-Cohen, S. (2003) *The Essential Difference: Men, Women and the Extreme Male Brain.* London: Penguin.

Grandin, T. (1996) *Thinking in Pictures and Other Reports from My Life with Autism.* London: Bloomsbury.

Hénault, I. (2006) *Asperger's Syndrome and Sexuality.* London: Jessica Kingsley Publishers.

Hendrickx, S. and Newton, K. (2007) *Asperger Syndrome – A Love Story.* London: Jessica Kingsley Publishers.

Holliday Willey, L. (2005) *Pretending to Be Normal.* London: Jessica Kingsley Publishers.

Ingudomnukul, E., Baron-Cohen, S., Wheelwright, S. and Knickmeyer, R. (2007) 'Elevated rates of testosterone-related disorders in women with autistic spectrum conditions.' *Hormones and Behaviour 51,* 5, 597–604.

Jacobs, B. (2006) *Loving Mr Spock.* London: Jessica Kingsley Publishers.

Lawson, W. (2005) *Sex, Sexuality and the Autistic Spectrum.* London: Jessica Kingsley Publishers.

Slater-Walker, G. and Slater-Walker, C. (2002) *An Asperger Marriage.* London: Jessica Kingsley Publishers.

Stanford, A. (2003) *Asperger Syndrome and Long-Term Relationships.* London: Jessica Kingsley Publishers.

Williams, D. (2003) *Exposure Anxiety – The Invisible Cage.* London: Jessica Kingsley Publishers.

Index